Easy Diabetic Meal Prep

Delicious and Healthy Recipes for Smart People on Diabetic Diet – 30 Days Meal Plan – The Code to Prevent and Reverse Diabetes.

By Mary Harper

Legal Disclaimer

The information contained in this book and its contents is not designed to replace any form of medical or professional advice; and is not meant to replace the need for independent medical, financial, legal, or other professional advice or services that may be required. The content and information in this book have been provided for educational and entertainment purposes only.

The content and information contained in this book have been compiled from sources deemed reliable, and they are accurate to the best of the Author's knowledge, information, and belief. However, the author cannot guarantee its accuracy and validity and therefore cannot be held liable for any errors and/or omissions. Further, changes are periodically made to this book as needed. Where appropriate and/or necessary, you must consult a professional (including but not limited to your doctor, attorney, financial advisor, or other such professional) before using any of the suggested remedies, techniques, and/or information in this book.

Upon using this book's contents and information, you agree to hold harmless the Author from any damages, costs, and expenses, including any legal fees, potentially resulting from the application of any of the information in this book. This disclaimer applies to any loss, damages, or injury caused by the use and application of this book's contents, whether directly or indirectly, whether for breach of contract, tort, negligence, personal injury, criminal intent, or under any other circumstance.

You agree to accept all risks of using the information presented in this book.

You agree that by continuing to read this book, where appropriate and/or necessary, you shall consult a professional (including but not limited to your doctor, attorney, financial advisor, or other such professional) before using any of the suggested remedies, techniques, or information in this book.

Table of Contents

Introduction

Have you ever been diagnosed by Diabetes or do you know someone who might a Diabetic and wants to find a way to help them? Well, this is the perfect book for you then!

Being diagnosed with Diabetes might be a little bit heartbreaking at first, but you'll soon realize that it isn't really the end of the world! In fact, there are thousands and thousands of individuals all around the world who have to lead a perfectly healthy life even after being diagnosed with Diabetes. The key to the heart of all is leading a healthy lifestyle and eating good food.

This book has been designed to act as a comprehensive guide to Diabetes that will teach you all the fundamentals of Diabetes and help you lead a healthy lifestyle with the hopes that you will be able to reverse your diabetes in the future!

Everything here is presented in a perfectly organized manner that will help you to easily navigate and study what you are looking for.

Once you are done with the intro, you can go in and explore the mouthwatering healthy recipes and learn how to come up with your very own meal plan!

Best of luck and Bon Appetite!

Chapter 1: The Basics Of Diabetes

What is Diabetes?

To fully understand the concept of Diabetes, it is important that you have a good understanding of how your body utilizes glucose and insulin and understand what they actually are.

So, let's first start with glucose.

Glucose is a form of sugar and is, generally speaking, the main source of energy, or "fuel" for our body. Whenever the body needs the energy to perform its day to day activities, it starts to burn glucose in order to get the required energy.

Glucose is formed in our body whenever the food that we eat gets broken down into various chemicals during digestion.

Glucose travels through the bloodstream and enters the cells in our body with the help of insulin.

Unlike Glucose though, Insulin is a type of hormone created in the pancreases. Simply put, it acts as a "Key" that allows cells to "open" up a pathway so that glucose can enter and provide the required energy.

Diabetes develops in the body whenever an insulin imbalance is created in the body. Or more specifically, when insulin runs in short supply/or is absent in our body.

When this happens, glucose is unable to enter the cells and as a result, more and more glucose stays in the bloodstream, which leads to the development of the condition known as Diabetes.

To be a bit more scientific, Diabetes is a disease that usually occurs the level of glucose in our blood (also known as blood sugar), spikes up to abnormal levels.

If Diabetes is not properly treated early on, then the blood glucose levels keep on rising, which leads to various health problems, including but not limited to blindness, kidney failure, limb amputation, nerve damage and so on.

While at present, there is no exact cure for Diabetes, it is still very much possible to lead a healthy and normal life with proper management and by eating the right kind of food.

The major 2 types of Diabetes

Currently, the well-established records indicate that there are two types of Diabetes, namely Type 2 and Type 1.

It should be noted that the Type 1 Diabetes was once known as Insulin Dependent Diabetes Mellitus or IDDM or even Juvenile-Onset Diabetes Mellitus. So, if you see any of those two words, don't be alarmed.

I will go into details for both types of Diabetes, however, to give you an overview.

When a person encounters Type- 1 Diabetes, the pancreas starts to experience an autoimmune attack where the body starts to harm itself, making the pancreas incapable of producing the ever so important hormone called "Insulin".

Studies have found a good number of anomalous antibodies in almost all patients suffering from Type – 1 Diabetes.

And just for your information, Antibodies are proteins in your bloodstream that help with the body's immune system.

Therefore, when a person suffers from Type – 1 Diabetes, he/she needs to rely on external medication to get the required amount of insulin.

That being said, now let's have a deeper look into the two different types of Diabetes.

First,

Type – 1

I have already given a brief about Type- 1 Diabetes above, so let's get into the technical details here.

Autoimmune diseases such as Type – 1 Diabetes cause the immune system of our body to accidentally produce anomalous inflammatory cells and antibodies that, instead of protecting the body, try to damage the healthy cells of the patient's body.

For Type -1, the beta cells found in the pancreas, which are specifically responsible for producing insulin, get attacked by these anomalous antibodies.

It is largely believed all around that the tendency to actually develop anomalous antibodies during Type -1 is inherited genetically. Though, the studies on this topic are still ongoing and not concrete.

It has been seen that exposure to various viral infections such as Coxsackie Virus or Mumps or various other environmental toxins might also be responsible to trigger the production of anomalous antibodies that might ultimately go and damage the beta cells of the pancreas.

Some of the most common antibodies seen in patients of Type-1 Diabetes include

- Anti-Glutamic Decarboxylase
- Anti-Insulin
- Anti Islet

Currently, the American Diabetes Association does not really recommend a general screening for individuals suffering from Type -1 Diabetes, however, individuals people who are seemingly at high risks, such as those having a first degree relative (such a parent or sibling) with diagnosed diabetes are highly encouraged to have themselves screened.

Recent studies have shown that Type-1 diabetes is more common in young ones, usually under the age of 30. However, older patients have also been seen to get affected by Type – 1.

The individuals who develop Diabetes at a very later stage of life fall into a subcategory of people who are said to have LADA or Latent Autoimmune Diabetes In Adults.

This basically means that they actually had diabetes from an earlier stage, but for some reason, it remained latent in their body.

LADA is very slow and in a way, progressive form of Diabetes (Type -1).

All in all though, currently only about 10% of the whole population suffering from diabetes tend to have Type 1, while the other 90% suffer from Type 2.

So, we are going to have a look at Type-2 next.

Type – 2

Non-Insulin Dependent Diabetes Mellitus (NIDDM) or even Adult- Onset Diabetes Mellitus are two of the scientific name that was previously used to describe Type-2 Diabetes.

A patient suffering from Type -2 Diabetes will still be able to produce insulin as the production does not completely come to a halt, however, the amount of insulin produced is significantly lower than the minimum amount require by the body to stay healthy.

In some cases though, the exact opposite might happen, resulting in the production of a large amount of insulin than that is required by the body!

One of the major caveats of Type-2 is that it basically makes the cells of the body particularly insensitive to insulin.

But that's not all, in addition to the problem mentioned above, the pancreas develops a form of insulin resistance that defects the release of insulin by the pancreas.

In fact, it has already been seen that a very steady decline of beta-cell insulin production happens in Type -1 that leads to even worse control of glucose in the bloodstream.

This is also one of the main reasons why patients with Type -2 Diabetes tend to undergo insulin therapy in the long run.

And lastly, the liver of patients suffering from Type-1 also starts to undergo Gluconeogenesis despite the already above normal levels of glucose in the bloodstream, which ultimately causes the liver to flood the bloodstream with even more glucose.

It is mostly believed that Type-2 primarily affects individuals who are over 30 years old, however, that's not necessarily true. While it is true that the possibility of getting the effect with Type-2 does increase with age, it is still seen that more and more teenagers are starting to develop Type-2 at a very early age.

Most of these cases are due to a lack of regular exercise, having higher than normal body weight, abnormal eating habits and so on.

Just as before, Genetic inheritance is also a major risk factor of Type 2, however, there are some others that you should be aware of as well. And the most significant one out of them is "Obesity". It has been seen that there is a very strong and direct relationship between the degree of obesity that a person is suffering from and the risk of developing Type-2. This is also why I have a chapter completely dedicated to explaining the basics of obesity.

And perhaps the worst part is that this is true for both young ones as well as adults. In fact, it has been estimated that the possibility of developing diabetes almost doubles for about a 20% increase over a body's normal desired weight.

As for age, data shows that for every 10 years in the crease after the age of 40, regardless of an individual's weight, the possibility of suffering from diabetes increases significantly.

The prevalence of diabetes is about 25% in individuals 65 years or older.

It has also been seen that the possibility of suffering from Type-2 varies from one ethnic group to the next as well.

For example, the prevalence rate is 7% In Non-Hispanic Caucasians while it is 8% in Asian Americans, 13% in Hispanics, 12.3% in Blacks and 20-50% in Native Americans.

The other types to know about

Apart from the ones mentioned above, there are some other types of diabetes that you should be aware of.

Secondary Diabetes

This type of diabetes refers to an abnormally elevated level of blood sugar happening from any other form of medical medication.

Secondary Diabetes might develop when an individual is suffering from pancreatic issues that may destroy the capacity of the pancreas to produce insulin. A quick example would be chronic pancreatitis.

Just in case you don't know, chronic pancreatitis essentially is the inflammation of your pancreas caused by toxins due to excess alcoholism. Other than that, surgical removal pancreas or certain types of trauma might also result in this.

Gestational Diabetes

It should be noted that Diabetes can actually happen for a temporary period of time during pregnancy. And in fact, it has been suggested that almost 2-10% of all pregnancies result in temporary diabetes.

During pregnancy, a great deal of hormonal changes takes place that might lead to a spike in blood sugar levels. Gestational Diabetes refers to this scenario when the blood sugar level elevates to abnormal levels during pregnancy due to hormonal changes. It does not last long though as Gestational Diabetes usually goes away after the birthing is complete.

Unfortunately, though, almost 35% - 60% of the women who suffer from gestational diabetes usually tend to develop type -2 after about 10-20 years of pregnancy. This is truer for individuals who required the injection of external insulin during pregnancy or those who fail to maintain their weight after delivery.

Women who are suspected to have gestational diabetes often are encouraged to take an oral glucose tolerance test around six weeks after delivery to ensure keep their diabetes in check and know if their gestational diabetes is developing into something more.

Hormonal Disturbances

Apart from that, Diabetes can also come from various types of hormonal disturbances. Excessive production of growth hormones alongside Cushing's syndrome might lead to diabetes.

In acromegaly (excess growth hormone production), the pituitary gland tends to cause excessive production of growth hormone that leads to hyperglycemia.

In Cushing's syndrome, on the other hand, the adrenal gland tends to lose control and produce a large amount of another hormone known as "Cortisol" that leads to increase blood sugar elevation as well.

Medication-related Diabetes

Apart from all of the scenarios mentioned above, you should know that Diabetes can also occur from various kinds of medications that might make your body to lose control of your diabetes or provoke latent diabetes to surface up.

Individuals who mostly take medications such as steroids or are taking medications to treat HIV are more at risk of developing diabetes.

The current state of Diabetes in U.S

And just in case you are wondering, you are a not alone victim either. In fact, in the U.S alone, it has been seen that more than 25 million Americans are suffering from diabetes.

Putting that into perspective, we are talking about almost 8.3% of the total population of the United States of America! And on top of that, One-Third of Americans who have diabetes aren't even aware of the fact that they are suffering from one, and the other third of Americans have what's "Prediabetes". People suffering from this condition have a blood glucose level higher than normal levels, but not yet as high as to be classified as Diabetes.

However, if they don't immediately start taking action, it is very much possible for prediabetes to turn into diabetes.

That being said though, the people who are overweight, it is extremely important that they incorporate a form of regular exercise in their life in order to help them keep their condition under check.

On the other hand, there are also certain types of medication that one might use in order to prevent diabetes.

So, as you can already understand, Diabetes isn't something that should be overlooked so easily. In fact, Diabetes is nothing short of an epidemic.

Why do you ask? Well, in large part, the rate of diabetes has increased because diets high in fat and calories and lack of exercise have led individuals to become obese, which is a major factor in diabetes.

This very same trend is seen all over the globe! As people in other countries are slowly becoming more and more affluent, they are at the same time becoming less active and are consuming richer yet malnutrition food.

All of these mean that the rate of diabetes is increasing rapidly as well! In fact, recent statistics claim that there will be almost 300 million people all over with diabetes by the year 2025, which is just a bit over 5 years away from now!

Learning to diagnose diabetes

Diagnosing if you have diabetes or not is actually easier than most people think. At present, there are two leading methods of diagnosing diabetes at home, which is testing your blood or an oral glucose test.

I will be talking a bit about both here.

First, let's talk about the blood glucose test.

Blood Glucose Test

So, when testing your blood glucose, a method called the "Fasting Blood Glucose" method is generally followed and is the preferred way to diagnose diabetes. It is extremely simple to do and convenient.

The core instruction here is to simply fast overnight (or for at least 8 hours), take a small sample of blood and analyze the blood.

This can be done easily at home using various portable devices, or you can visit a doctor or diagnostics lab to have it checked.

If you are doing at home, what you must understand is:

- Normal levels for plasma glucose should be less than 100 mg/dl
- Glucose levels more than 126 mg/dl on more than two different occasions indicate diabetes
- And lastly, a random test (without fasting) that gives a count of 200 mg/dl or more indicates diabetes too.

Oral Glucose Tolerance Test

This method is not really used routinely these days, but the OGTT is pretty much the best when it comes to diagnosing Type-2 Diabetes.

It is still regularly used for checking individuals with symptoms of gestational diabetes.

For the Oral Test, a person is required to fast overnight (at least 8 or a maximum of 16 hours).

Once that is done, the first step is to check the person for the fasting glucose. Once that, the person is given an oral dose (about 75gm) or glucose. Afterwhich, the blood is taken at several intervals.

Keep in mind that there are various other methods deployed by obstetricians, but the one mentioned above is considered to be the standard one.

There are certain steps that one should take though before taking the test, those are:

- It is essential that the person is in good health
- It is essential that the person is active
- It should be checked that the person is not taking any medicine that might affect the blood glucose levels
- On the day of the test, the individual should not indulge in any form of drinking or smoking, not even coffee.

The original version of the Oral Test used to measure the level of blood glucose 5 times over a long session of 3 hours.

Some physicians, on the other hand, tend to get a baseline sample that is followed by just another sample about 2 hours later from the time of drinking the glucose drink.

For an individual who has no diabetes, the level of glucose will immediately spike after the drink and then drop rapidly.

For people with diabetes, the levels will rise up to an abnormal level and stay there.

To summarize the results:

- If a person has a glucose level that is less than 140mg/dl after 2 hours from taking the glucose solution, with the level less than 200 mg/dl during the 2 hours the person is said to have a normal response.
- If a person has a glucose level that is less than 126mg/dl after 2 hours from taking the glucose solution, with the level hovering around 140-199 mg/dl during the 2 hours, the person is said to have an impaired glucose tolerance.
- If two diagnostics test done on two different days shows a high glucose result, then the person has diabetes
- In the case of pregnant women, a fasting glucose level of 92 mg/dl, after an hour a level of 180 mg/dl and after 2 hours a level of 153 mg/dl would dictate that the women have gestational diabetes.

The symptoms of Diabetes

Checking your blood or having an oral test aren't the only two ways how you can check your Diabetes. There are certain signs and symptoms that you should keep an eye out for, that might imply that you have Diabetes.

The most common ones are:

For Type 1:
- Patches of dark skin, round neck or armpits
- Being frequently affected by infection
- Delayed healing of sores
- Having a blurry vision
- Constant fatigue
- Unwanted loss of weight
- Constantly increased hunger
- Increase urination
- Constant sensation of thirst

For Type 2:
- Unwanted weight loss
- Numbness or sensation of pain in feet/hand
- Bruises might take longer to heal
- The extreme level of fatigue
- Increase urination
- The feeling of constant hunger
- Blurred vision

Maintaining stress related to diabetes

When you are suffering from diabetes, it is pretty normal to be stressed out a bit all the time. This might lead you to skip meals or even forgetting your medication, which might affect the level of glucose in your blood.

But, you need to understand that life is full of hurdles and setbacks, you really can't let them hold you back.

In that light, here are six tips that should help you keep your stress under control:

- Make sure to take some time to just relax and unwind. Try to practice deep breathing, visualization, meditation or even muscle relaxation. All of these will help you to stay calm and keep your body healthy.

- Make sure to involve yourself in regular exercise. Take a hike, ride a bicycle or just simply take a jog. They all help. And if those aren't your thing, then you can always go for something more soothing like tai chi or yoga.

- When you are feeling too stressed, try to call up a friend or a beloved family member and talk to them. And if that's not helping, you can always take help from a psychiatrist/counselor.

- Try to accept the things that are not under your control and you can't change. Trying to enforce a change on something that is not within your reach will only make things worse for you. Better advice is to look for better ways of handling the situation instead of trying to change it.

- Don't put too much pressure on you, try to be good to yourself and don't expect much. You are a human being after all right? You can make mistakes, accept that. Just try your best.

- And lastly, always try to maintain a positive attitude. Even when things go completely wrong, try to see the good instead of the bad and focus on that. Try to find things in all phases of your life that make you happy and that you appreciate it. Your friends, work, health and family for example. You have no idea how much of help just a simple change of perspective can bring.

Is it possible to reverse Diabetes?

Now, this is the million-dollar question, isn't it? Assuming that you are already affected by Diabetes, is it possible to reverse it or cure it completely?

Well, the answer to the latter is, unfortunately, a no at the moment, as there is currently no way to completely cure your Diabetes, but it is possible to manage it and lead a healthy life.

And following that, comes the next issue, reversing it.

Studies have actually shown that there are multiple ways through which you can reverse your diabetes. Does that mean you will be completely cured? Not really, but reversing it would mean that despite having Diabetes, your blood sugar levels will still stay at a very respectable healthy limit.

The signs and symptoms might return later on, but with proper maintenance, it is possible to pass years and years of healthy days.

Now comes the next question, how can you actually reverse it?

Well, there are actually a number of different ways of doing this.

Special Diets

I have dedicated a complete chapter to this. There are various types of diets that you can follow in order to keep your diabetes under control. I have talked about the most common one in one of the following chapters.

And just to solidify my point further, a recent study has shown that a low-calorie diet is actually extremely effective in keeping diabetes under check.

During the concerned study, two individuals were asked to follow a very low-calorie diet (625-850) per day diet for about 2 to 5 months. Which was then followed by a restricted plan that was designed to help them lose weight.

In the end, it was noticed that the individuals who took part in this program had their diabetes reversed by lowering down the blood glucose level to almost normal levels that lasted for at least six months to about a year.

Exercise

Apart from special diets, physical activity is another way through which you can improve the condition of your diabetes.

This might a little bit tough to do if you are alone, but it is very much possible. However, you should keep in mind that working out alone won't help you, you must work out and follow a well balanced healthy diet.

Both of these combined will go to great lengths to help you lose weight and control your diabetes.

In fact, a study has shown that people who try to complete 10,1000 steps per day and work out for about 2 and a ½ hours every week, while cutting down 500-800 calories per day, and follow a proper diet routine, have a 50% chance of lowering down the blood sugar to normal levels.

Bariatric Surgery

For those of you who don't know, this is a type of surgery that encourages you to trim down weight by putting an artificial limiter in your digestive system and stomach and letting you control how much you can eat.

Apart from helping you lost weight, this will help you to reverse diabetes as well. The theory is that this surgery also affects the hormones present in your intestines that help to control your blood glucose level.

Researches indicate that almost 3 quarters of people all over tend to see a decrease in their levels of diabetes after gastric sleeve, gastric bypass or bariatric surgery.

But keep in mind that this is a pretty significant surgery that has certain risks, so make sure to talk to your personal physician before taking any drastic step. But to end on a positive note, most individuals who took this surgery were able to reverse diabetes.

Fasting

Fasting is possibly one of the most practical and logical ways of losing weight. Mainly because it is extremely straight forward, however, you should know that this is not a mainstream method to reverse Type-2.

A relatively small study has shown that therapeutic fasting (not having drinks or food for a specific amount of time) can actually help to reverse the symptoms of diabetes.

Three individuals were involved in an experiment where they were asked to follow a program that involved 3 days of 24 hours fast each week for a number of months.

The result? Two of the three individuals were able to completely let go of their medications while the third individual was able to partially let go of their medicines. But within just a matter of weeks, all three of the subjects were able to keep their blood glucose level in check without taking insulin!

Another study shows that eating 500-600 calories for about 2 days a week and following a normal diet on the other days helped individuals with Type -2 diabetes lower down their blood glucose levels to a greater degree.

If are interested in trying out fasting, make sure to consult with your personal physician before embarking on a fasting journey.

Looking deeply in Obesity

So, as you can already tell, Obesity is one of the core factors that contribute to Diabetes. Let us understand that in more detail now.

In strictly general terms, Obesity is a physical condition which a person faces when he/she has gathered an unusual level of fat in their body. Such high levels of fat often lead to the body experiencing severe negative effects on the heart and health as a whole.

At the moment of writing, nearly 2 in every 3 adults in America were found to suffer from Obesity, which pretty rounds it up to 68.8% if the population being obese.

The measurement of how much obese a person can come from a calculation made to figure out the BMI (Body Mass Index) of a person. It is generally considered that if the bodyweight of a person is 20% greater than the estimated value, then he/she is obese.

Understand the Body Mass Index

Strictly speaking, BMI is a measurement that is derived by considering the height and weight of a person. The calculate BMI is them compared to a table through which a rough idea of the person's physique is acquired. Generally, the formula below is used

$$\text{Body Mass Index} = \frac{\text{Weight (in kg)}}{\text{Height}^2 \text{ (in m)}}$$

Once the Index has been obtained, a similar chart to the one below is observed in order to assess the results.

BMI Chart

Underweight | Healthy | Overweight | Obese | Extremely obese

Weight lbs	100	105	110	115	120	125	130	135	140	145	150	155	160	165	170	175	180	185	190	195	200	205	210	215
kgs	45.5	47.7	50.0	52.3	54.5	56.8	59.1	61.4	63.6	65.9	68.2	70.5	72.7	75.0	77.3	79.5	81.8	84.1	86.4	88.6	90.9	93.2	95.5	97.7
Hight in/cm																								
5'0" - 152.4	19	20	21	22	23	24	25	26	27	[illegible]	[illegible]	[illegible]	[illegible]	[illegible]	[illegible]	[illegible]	[illegible]	[illegible]	[illegible]	[illegible]	[illegible]	40	41	42
5'1" - 154.9	18	19	20	21	22	23	24	25	26	27	[illegible]	[illegible]	[illegible]	[illegible]	[illegible]	[illegible]	[illegible]	[illegible]	[illegible]	[illegible]	[illegible]	[illegible]	[illegible]	40
5'2" - 157.4	18	19	20	21	22	22	23	24	25	26	27	28	29	30	31	[illegible]	[illegible]	[illegible]	[illegible]	[illegible]	[illegible]	[illegible]	[illegible]	[illegible]
5'3" - 160.0	17	18	19	20	21	22	23	24	24	25	26	27	28	[illegible]	[illegible]	[illegible]	[illegible]	[illegible]	[illegible]	[illegible]	[illegible]	[illegible]	[illegible]	[illegible]
5'4" - 162.5	17	18	18	19	20	21	22	23	24	24	25	26	27	28	29	[illegible]	[illegible]	[illegible]	[illegible]	[illegible]	[illegible]	[illegible]	[illegible]	[illegible]
5'5" - 165.1	16	17	18	19	20	20	21	22	23	24	25	[illegible]	[illegible]	[illegible]	[illegible]	[illegible]	[illegible]	[illegible]	[illegible]	[illegible]	[illegible]	[illegible]	[illegible]	[illegible]
5'6" - 167.6	16	17	17	18	19	20	21	21	22	23	24	25	26	26	27	28	[illegible]	[illegible]	[illegible]	[illegible]	[illegible]	[illegible]	[illegible]	[illegible]
5'7" - 170.1	16	16	17	18	18	19	20	21	22	22	23	24	25	26	26	27	28	29	[illegible]	[illegible]	[illegible]	[illegible]	[illegible]	[illegible]
5'8" - 172.7	15	16	16	17	18	19	19	20	21	22	22	23	24	25	25	26	27	28	[illegible]	[illegible]	[illegible]	[illegible]	[illegible]	[illegible]
5'9" - 175.2	14	15	16	17	17	18	19	20	20	21	22	22	23	24	25	26	26	27	[illegible]	[illegible]	[illegible]	[illegible]	[illegible]	[illegible]
5'10" - 177.8	14	15	15	16	17	18	18	19	20	20	21	22	23	23	24	25	26	26	27	[illegible]	[illegible]	[illegible]	[illegible]	[illegible]
5'11" - 180.3	14	14	15	16	16	17	18	18	19	20	21	21	22	23	23	24	25	[illegible]	[illegible]	[illegible]	[illegible]	[illegible]	[illegible]	[illegible]
6'0" - 182.8	13	14	14	15	16	17	17	18	19	19	20	21	21	22	23	23	24	25	25	26	27	27	28	29
6'1" - 185.4	13	13	14	15	15	16	17	17	18	19	19	20	21	21	22	23	23	24	25	25	26	27	27	28
6'2" - 187.9	12	13	14	14	15	16	16	17	18	18	19	19	20	21	21	22	23	23	24	25	25	26	27	27
6'3" - 190.5	12	13	13	14	15	15	16	16	17	18	18	19	20	20	21	21	22	23	23	24	25	25	26	26
6'4" - 193.0	12	12	13	14	14	15	15	16	17	17	18	18	19	20	20	21	22	22	23	23	24	25	25	26

The factors that contribute to Obesity

The first thing that comes to mind when thinking about the causes of Obesity is definitely food-related. But that's not really where everything ends as there are more factors that largely contribute to obesity alongside a heavy diet. Some of the more essential ones which you should know about are:

- **A general lack of energy balance:** This is true. If the energy input and out of your life is not balanced properly, then you will start gaining weight. The equation goes something like this:
  - Same energy input and Same energy output = no weight change
  - More energy input and less output = weight increases
  - More energy output and less energy input = Weight decreases

  And where is the energy coming from? Excessive amounts of food and drinks of course!
- **A result of your gene:** Yes, to a large extent, obesity is a condition that might be heavily influenced by genes passed on from your parents or ancestor. The offsprings are obese parents are more like to suffer from obesity in the future, when compared to those of leaner parents.
- **The volley of junk food:** The days of using natural food ingredients is almost gone! Every now and then you are faced with a product that is excessively deliciously, yet is complete made using chemicals and artificial produces. These "Hyperpalatable" junk foods take a huge toll on our bodies.
- **Food Addiction:** Linking from the "Hyperpalatable" junk foods. Some people often get addicted to these foods, since they are both delicious and cheap. This is in fact certified as a very complex medical

issue to deal with and from a biological standpoint, it is very tough to overcome.

- **Lack of Sleep:** This might come as a surprise to our "Night Owl" readers. But this is, in fact, something which should be considered. Recent studies performed at the University of Warwick have shown that people who tend to sleep less are prone to suffer from obesity much more in the future.
- **Medications:** Sleeplessness in combination with a high functioning lifestyle often influences people to go for various pharmaceutical drugs such as antidepressants and anti-psychotics. These drugs have the tendency to alter the working mechanism of the brain by forcing it to store more fat rather than burning it.
- **Pregnancy:** This is a natural process of life. As you get older the muscles of your body will tend to give away and become loose. If you don't maintain a properly healthy and active lifestyle, then weight gain is inevitable. For women, however, it should be kept in mind that after menopause (and pregnancy) women usually gain about 5 pounds. If this is not toned down in the future, it might lead to obesity.

These are just some of the important but crucial issues which you should keep in mind.

Now we know some of the reasons, let's see how we can start preparing ourselves for our journey ahead.

Chapter 2: Learning to be sugar-free

If you have gone through the book up until now, you probably have understood that glucose and in turn "Sugary" foods are one of the core culprits that might lead an individual to develop diabetes.

So, this chapter focuses a bit on teaching you how you can slowly incorporate a "Sugar" free lifestyle to your daily routine.

To be more specific, we are talking about "Detoxing" your body of sugar.

What is a Detox?

Before going into explaining a Detox, let's talk a little bit about the process of detoxification.

Generally speaking, detoxification is a process that our body performs on a regular basis to keep the body free from harmful chemicals known as "toxins".

Now these toxins are generally divided into two different categories

- **Endotoxins:** These are the molecules that are made inside the body as byproducts of the body's regular metabolism.
- **Exotoxins:** These are the molecules that are introduced to the body by an external means. They can come through eating, breathing, drinking or through skin absorption.

Examples of Endotoxins include lactic acid, urea and microbe waste products. Alternatively, examples of Exotoxins include pesticides, pollutants, tobacco chemicals, mercury in seafood, car exhaust lead and air pollution, etc.

Since all of these toxins are possess the ability to greatly hamper the normal working condition of the body and potentially damage human health, the body tends to regularly get rid of these through various means such as through defecation, urination, respiration, and sweat.

It should be noted that the effectiveness of detoxification varies from person to person. This is due to the fact that the process of detoxification largely depends on the diet, lifestyle, environment health status and a number of different genetic factors.

Safe to say, that all of these different factors greatly vary from one person to the next, which ultimately influences the effectiveness of the detoxification process.

However, it should be noted that in some circumstances the level of toxins in the body might increase to such a level that the body is unable to get rid of them properly. Such situations tend to greatly hamper a body's health in multiple ways.

- They might give you blurry vision
- They might influence memory loss
- They might cause disorders in the central nervous system
- They might increase the risk of breast cancer
- It might lead to unexplained weight gain
- It may lead to lost testosterone levels in men

- It might lead to joint inflammation
- It might increase the risk of colon cancer

To tackle such circumstances, various Detox programs are designed to prevent the body from being overexposed to a certain type of toxin.

Detox programs often require people to get rid of processed foods or a specific type of foods such as dairy, eggs, gluten, red meat or peanuts and so on.

In our case, we will be focusing on a "Sugar Detox", which specifically requires a person to get rid of sugar from his/her diet.

Starting to Detox

To start off, below are the very first steps that you should take in order to start your detoxification journey.

- **Water down excess sugar intake:** This is very important and you should start off your journey by doing this. This can be looked at as a seasonal detox that will help you increase your overall health and metabolism.
- **Drink more and more water:** Water, the essence of life. Starting this day, you should encourage yourself to drink as much water as you can. In fact, starting off your day with a tall glass of water just a tint of lemon helps to completely rehydrate the
- **Don't remain static:** Even though this might be tough for some individuals considering the amount of time they have. But it is highly recommended to make a schedule to do some daily exercise. It not only helps to get lean, but it also aids blood circulation and improves the lymphatic system. It is also said that it helps to improve digestion, lubricate joints and increase the overall strength of the body.
- **Go for the Tea:** Especially Green Tea is possible. These are awesome herbal solutions to detoxify your body and keep you hydrated at the same time.
- **Try to go for Organic food:** Try to keep your food palate full of fruits and vegetables of various colors. These are full of macronutrients that your body will require and will take you to great distances in the long run.
- **Try to avoid environmental pollution:** Easier said than done. This is almost impossible to do! Given the level of pollution and allergens all around us. However, it is highly advised that you always flush your nasal pathway using a Neti Pot which will greatly help you to eliminate the side effects of air pollutants and help you to breathe normally.
- **Go for Sauna every now and then:** Sweating as much as possible is a great way to detoxify your body. And what better way to sweat while meditating rather than going for a Sauna bath!? Every now and then you should take some time out just for yourself and get for a Sauna bath. You will leave the room completely refreshed.
- **Scrub the dirt off:** Spiders tend to shed their skin whenever possible to rejuvenate themselves. Humans can do the same, albeit in

a less scary way! You should always take some time to brush your skin and undergo oil massages to fully exfoliate the toxins from your outer skin and refresh yourself.

Advantages of Sugar Detox

- It helps to get rid of your junk food addiction and keeps your body free from the harmful exotoxins.
- It will greatly help you to feel satisfied (you won't feel hungry from time to time) and will have greater control over what you eat and whatnot.
- Since you will be cutting down on overpriced processed junk foods, you will be able to save a whole lot of money.
- It will help you to get rid of symptoms such as fatigue, digestive issues, achiness, allergies, headaches, and brain fogginess.
- It will help you to trim down your excess body fat.
- It will increase your sex drive and give you a more fulfilling sexual experience

The 8-week strategy to help you cut back on your sugar craving

Throughout the discussion I had with you up until now, you should have a clear grasp of what a Sugar Detox Diet and how it can benefit your health and life overall.

But the main problem that most newcomers face is the lack of having proper guidelines to follow.

They get confused on how to work their way up the ladder, and ultimately fail to successfully get rid of the habit. To make things easier, in this section I will be outlining a very simple 8 weeks guideline that will greatly help any interested individual to get rid of their sugar temptation in no time!

Week 1

The first week is somewhat of a preparatory session for the upcoming weeks. Things are not that much complicated here, all you have to do is try to cut down on as much sugar as you can. Some cutbacks that you can go for are

- Start to use avocado slices with some olive oil, instead of jam
- Go for eggs on a toast instead of low-fat yogurt/ granola
- Go for soda water or herbal tea instead of soft drinks
- When at the movies, avoid bag of candy's and go for popcorn
- Don't go for any heavy desert at night, go for a simple Cheese
- If you have the habit of drinking tea with a good amount of sugar, then simply halve the amount of sugar, and if possible then add a bit more milk/artificial sweetener
- Alternatively, if you are addicted to soft drinks, then go for a diet version of them

Week 2

Since you are starting to deprive your body of certain foods, in the second week you might experience some drawback effect and your temptation for seeking out food will increase. This week, you are going to need to find an alternative for sugar, so you should opt for

- More proteins and unprocessed fat such as eggs, nuts, coconuts, and cheese

Week 3

This week you are going to give your body a slight break and introduce a little bit of sweetness back to your diet. This phase is often known as going "Cold Turkey"

Here you will go for

- Fresh and dried fruits and juices
- Granola and granola bars
- Sugar-free jams
- Condiments such as BBQ sauce, balsamic vinegar, and tomatoes
- Various flavored yogurts
- Honey
- Agave
- Coconut sugar and palm
- Soft drinks, chocolate, etc.

Week 4

This week, you will start to set back on your diet again. You are completely going to eliminate fructose from your diet, so

- Go away from any kinds of fruit juice

Week 5

For this week, you are to keep two things in mind. Try to get rid of any kind of alternative sweetness from your life. So, try to refrain from any kind of sweeteners.

Alternatively, you are to also apply the 20 minutes rule.

- So, no alternative sweeteners.
- Whenever you start to face serious cravings, try to calm yourself down, sip some tea and give yourself 20 minutes to allow the temptation to calm down.

There are few things that you should keep in mind for this week though. Some tips to be exact.

- **When getting a sugar temptation in Mid-Morning:** Go for a little sugar-free breakfast
- **When getting a sugar temptation in the afternoon:** Try to go out for a walk and do some chores. Alternatively, you may also want to go for a few sips of tea.
- **When getting a sugar temptation while with friends:** Try to ignore them and go for a large pot of chai or tea.
- **When getting a sugar temptation after dinner:** Go for cheese as alternatives to deserts. Have a bath and read some books.

I have already mentioned that during the first few weeks, you might face some issues such as dizziness, nauseous feeling and so on.

Tackle them by

- Drinking a whole lot of warm water
- Go for acupuncture treatment
- Go for a Sauna
- Try some herbal alternatives
- Ingest Calcium and Magnesium
- Increase your Green Tea intake
- Try to go for 1 teaspoon of cinnamon per day

Week 6

By now things might start to become a little bland in terms of flavor, so this week we will be focusing on some flavors.

- Add a bit of fruit to your diet. Try to stick to low or medium fructose fruits.
- Low fructose such as kiwis, honeydew lemon, grapefruit, raspberries and blueberries
- Medium fructose fruit such as plums, oranges, and strawberries
- High-fructose fruits such as grapes, apples, mangoes, cherries, bananas are to be avoided
- As for flavors, you can add ingredients like
    - Vanilla powder
    - Cinnamon
    - Licorice root
    - Almond milk
    - Sautéed onion
    - Roast vegetables
    - Sweet sugar-free drinks

Week 7

If you have survived week 6, then you are already a survivor. But with this week, you might start to lapse a bit. The following tips will help you to prevent that from happening

- Go for some yoga classes, take a swim
- Try to eat some nutrition-rich food, making sure that you don't go astray from protein, fats, and vegetables, keep in mind that you are to avoid any kind of starchy carb for at least one day of the week.
- Try to opt for coconut produces such as coconut juice, smoothies, flakes, ice cream, etc.

Week 8

With almost 60 days of sugar-free struggle, you can finally call yourself a certified Sugar-Detox!

However, from this point on, you should try to maintain your new-found routine and stick to the sugar-free way. You are now technically off the training wheels and are on your own. However, here are some tips that might help you

- Try to look at sugar from a different perspective and appreciate the changes that you have undergone, both physically and mentally.
- Always try to keep experimenting with different sugar-free foods and lapse fixes. Don't be afraid to fail, but always get back up.
- Always stay up-to-date with all of the latest news surrounding the world of sugar-detox diets and keep yourself attached to online communities with likeminded people.
- Don't overdo on the fat.
- Try to keep your daily sugar intake as low as 3-6% if absolutely necessary.
- Go for about 1-2 servings of fruit (comprised of mostly berries)
- As something of a treat, you may add a bit of 85% chocolate occasionally.

If done right, then the whole process should help you a lot to keep your diabetes in check.

Chapter 3: The Basics of Meal Plan

There is a very well-known quote that has been hovering around the ears of men and weapon since the early days

"Failing to prepare, it Preparing to Fail"

Even though this sentence seems like a very simple collection of words, it actually holds a very deep and elaborate meaning.

To explain, the sentence explicitly focuses on the fact that without proper preparation, it is pretty much confirmed that you won't be able to win any battles of your life.

And we are not talking about battles with guns and ammo! Rather, we are talking about the daily battles which we face.

Going into an exam, going to give the next presidential speech and even deciding to go on a diet! Without proper preparation or practice, you are bound to fail in all of those.

Please do pardon my slightly pessimistic intro! I am not talking about these just to discourage, rather, I want you to understand just how important preparation is to any victory.

Incidentally, the same concept is very much true when it comes to cooking!

Meal Prepping is one of the most important, yet highly ignored aspect of any diet. And this is even truer for an individual who leads a very busy life and finds it rather difficult to take off some time in order to create healthy and edible meals.

That being said, in this introductory chapter, I will be going through the basics of Meal Prep and teach you, how you can properly set up everything for your Meal Prep journey.

Exploring the Meal Prepping Concept

Perhaps in the simplest term, the main objective of Meal Prepping is to essentially create a blueprint of how you are going to conduct and incorporate the diet that you are following. Even if you are not following a diet! You can create a rough meal plan for the whole week.

Dissecting the concept even further, we are able to get the definition below:

"Meal Prepping is the process of planning what you are going to eat (and how you are going to make it) ahead of time."

Why should one Meal Prep?

And if you are wondering as to why you should pursue Meal Prep, well...

- It helps you to save a lot of money by allowing you to set up a rough estimate of your food budget ahead of time
- If allows you to stick to a healthy plan and eat as much healthy food as possible
- It minimizes food wastage
- It clears off the burden of "What you should cook next" and eases your mind, clearing it up of any food-related stress.

- Prevent the wasting of time by letting you know exactly "What" you are going to eat and "When".
- Help you avoid monotony in your daily meal by spicing up the routine from time to time.

How does a Diabetic benefit from Meal Prep?

Well apart from all the benefits mentioned above, having a well organized and thought out plan will help you to keep your blood sugar levels in check. This, in turn, will help you manage your weight and decrease the possibility of your heart being affected by heart diseases by controlling your fat input and blood pressure.

If you are not following a properly designed meal plan, you might end up consuming excess calories and fat, which causes your blood glucose level to spike up.

And as you already know now, if you are blood glucose level is not kept in check, it might lead to hyperglycemia that might even lead to kidney, nerve or heart damages.

A meal plan helps to keep your blood glucose at safe levels by encouraging healthy food habits.

Asides from keeping you healthy, a well-planned meal plan will also help you to trim down excess weight and prevent obesity, which is one of the major factors of Type-2 Diabetes.

So, it's safe to say that in the long run, whether you are diabetic or a prediabetic, following a proper meal plan will definitely help you achieve your health goal. And the best part is that, once you understand the core concepts of meal prep, you can incorporate them into any diet program you like!

Preparing your Kitchen For Meal Prepping

If you are jumping into the world of Meal Prep for the first time you might feel a bit confused as to how you should prepare your kitchen.

These are some of the staples that you should keep around in your kitchen.

Cutting Boards: Try to get boards that are made from solid materials such as plastic, glass, rubber or marble! These are mostly corrosion-resistant and the non-porous surface makes it easier to clean them than wood.

Tools and Equipment: the most basic ones include

Measuring cups: Required to measure out spices and condiments.

Various sized spoons: The multiple sized spoons will allow you to measure out small amounts of spices.

Glass bowls and non-metallic containers: They are required for storing the meat alongside marinade.

Packaging materials (mentioned above): The materials are mentioned above and they can be used to store the meat in the fridge.

Kitchen and paper towels: These are required draining the meat.

Cold Storage Space (the fridge will suffice): Since the meats are required to be kept under 40 degrees Fahrenheit, a fridge should be enough.

Knives: Sharp knives should be used to slice the meat accordingly. While using the knife, you should keep the following in mind.
- Always make sure to use a sharp knife
- Never hold a knife under your arm or leave it under a piece of meat
- Always keep your knives within visible distance
- Always keep your knifepoint down
- Always cut down towards the cutting surface and away from your body
- Never allow children to toy with knives unattended
- Wash the knives while cutting different types of food

Mesh glove for protection: Cutting the meat requires precision as you will be using a very sharp knife. The following types of gloves should be kept in mind:
- **Rubber gloves**
- **Butchering Gloves**
- **Mesh Glove**

Kitchen Scale for measurement: A kitchen scale will allow you to get accurate measurements of slightly pieces of meat and condiments.

Internal Thermometer: A meat thermometer will help you to measure the internal temperature of the jerky to ensure that you are able to ensure that the jerky is ready.

Baking Sheet: These are a flat, rectangular metal pan that is used in the oven, mainly for flat products such as sheet cakes, cookies, etc.

Colander: A colander is a bowl-shaped kitchen utensil with holes that allows you to drain food such as pasta or rice. These are also used to rinsed veggies.

Aluminum Foil: Also known as misnomer tin foil, these are used to wrap up and cover food.

The Different Time Saving Cooking Methods

If you don't buy expensive appliances such as the Instant Pot, Air Fryer or Crock-Pot, the following cooking methods should help you to stay ahead of the pack and save a lot of time.

- **Grilling:** This method is the best to use when cooking tender cuts of fish or meat. The grill should be well heated before cooking. Some meats such as bacon, sausage already contain enough fat for grilling, for other cuts such as chicken breast, you will need to baste them with a bit of oil or cooking liquid.
- **Griddling:** This is also known as "Char-Grilling" and the method requires the user to cook in a ridged cast-iron pan on high heat that quickly sears the food on the outside. This method is not only fast but healthy as well! Griddling is ideal for thin cuts such as chops, poultry breast fillets, steaks, seafood as well as thick slices of summer veggies such as zucchini or eggplant.

- **Stir-Frying:** Lean cuts are perfect for stir-frying as are other firm-textured fish and shellfish noodles, rice and vegetables. Since this process allows for quick cooking, all the color, nutrients and flavor of the ingredients are preserved almost to perfection.
- **Steaming:** Food is steamed above simmering water. In this case, the natural flavor, shape, color, and texture alongside all water-soluble vitamins and minerals are retained perfectly.
- **Microwaving:** While microwaves may have an ill reputation amongst foodies, every kitchen needs one! If you are busy, foods can be prepared or re-heated in a fraction of the time it would take to cook following other conventional methods.

Amazing Meal Prep Ideas

Keep in mind that the following are just a few of the hundreds of different Meal Prep ideas you can scrape up from the deepest corners of your brain! These are to merely give you an idea of what you can truly do and how you can start organizing your dietary regime.

Make a plan ahead of time: This is really important and the first step that you should do when practicing meal prep is to make a habit of planning your meals as early as possible. Early on, it is best recommended that you create meal plans of perhaps 2-3 days and increase the number as you become more experienced.

Keep a good supply of mason jars: When considering the healthy salad, Mason jars are absolutely amazing! It is a good idea to prepare your salad and store them in mason jars ahead of time. While doing this though, make sure to keep the salad dressing at the bottom as they might make the greens soggy.

Three-way seasoning in one pan: If your diet requires you to stick with lean meats such as chicken, then seasoning them from time to time might become somewhat of a chore. A simple solution to that is to prepare a pan with aluminum foil dividers. Using these will allow you to season three or more (depending on how many dividers you are using) types of chicken seasoning to be done using the same pan!

Boil eggs in an oven instead of a pot: Boiling an egg following the traditional method is a lengthy and slow process, a good way to boil a bunch of eggs is to use your oven! Take a muffin tin and rimmed baking sheet and fill it up with water, add a dozen of eggs and boil them all in one go!

Keep your prepared smoothies frozen in muffin tins: Plopping out a number of different ingredients early in the morning might be a chore for some people. A simple solution to that is to go ahead and freeze up your blended smoothies in muffin tins. This will not only save up time but will also give you a delicious dose of satisfaction as you wake up in the morning and toss a few "smoothie cups" into the blender for a simple yet healthy breakfast.

Roast vegetables that require the same time in one batch: If your meal plan requires a large number of veggies to be prepared, divide the veggies according to the time taken for them boil/roast and prepare the veggies in the same batch in one go! For example, you can create a batch of rapid cooking vegetables such as mushrooms, asparagus or cherry tomatoes and a batch of slow-roasting veggies such as potatoes, cauliflowers, and carrots in order to minimize time loss and maximize output. This will save a lot of time and make things more efficient.

Learn to effectively use a skewer: When you think of skewers, you automatically think of kabobs! But Skewers aren't necessarily designed to be used only with street meats. Wooden skewers can actually help you to measure how much meat you are going to consume in one go. So, you can punch in your meat in multiple skewers and divide them evenly and store them for the rest of the week. When the time comes, just take out one skewer and cook it up!

Keep a good supply of sectioned plastic containers: Containers are extremely important it comes to meal prepping! Keep as many as you can, and if possible go for "Sectioned" ones as you will be able to keep the ingredients separated from each other in the same box. It will prevent making a mess and save space.

Keep a tab of your accomplishments: This is perhaps the most essential aspect of a Meal Prepping routine. Always make sure to somehow measure your progress and set small milestones for you to accomplish. Achieving these milestones will encourage you and inspire you further to keep pushing yourself until you reach your final goal. Alternatively, looking at your positive progress will greatly motivate you to push forward as well!

Common Mistakes To Avoid

We all make mistakes; it is a part of human nature. But there are some common mistakes that are made by individuals during the early days of Meal Prepping.

To ensure that you do not make the same mistakes, let me outline a few!

- Don't keep your food for too long out as they might very easily get contaminated with germs or bacteria,
- Don't rush when washing and rinsing your vegetables. Putting a little time there won't destroy your daily routine! Take your time and thoroughly wash your vegies before processing them.
- You should always make sure that you are heating your foods properly. Overheating them will burn them up while not heating them enough will leave harmful bacteria on the surface of the food. Use a meat thermometer if possible when dealing with meats.

Food Safety

Preventing contamination while handling the different ingredients is very important when it comes to prepping your ingredients for a meal plan!

Keeping that in mind, let me give you some time as to how you can keep your veggies and meat as safe and healthy as possible.

Vegetables: It is extremely important that you wash all of your vegetables and fruits before you eat them in order to ensure that they are safe to eat!

Washing will help you to remove bacteria that may have come with the vegetable as make it safe to eat.

Generally speaking, the bacteria are usually found in the soil where the veggie was grown, so you should wash in such a way so that no soil sticks to the body.

When washing the vegetables, wash them under a running tap and rub them well with tap water.

A good way is to take a bowl of fresh water and rinse them thoroughly.

Make sure to start with the least soiled ones first and give them a final rinse before cooking.

Washing loose produce is particularly important as they tend to have more soil attached to them than pre-packed fruits and vegetables.

Another good way is to peel the skin off the fruits and veggies if possible to make them cleaner.

Asides from washing the veggies themselves, the following tips will help you to prevent cross-contamination of vegetables

- Always make sure to wash your hands before handling raw food
- Store the raw food and the ones that are processed separately
- Use different chopping foods for raw food and the ones that are processed for eating
- Make sure to always clean your knives

Meat: If you can make sure to follow the steps below, you will be able to ensure that your meat is safe from any kind of bacterial or airborne contamination.

This first step is very much essential as no market bought or freshly cut meat is completely sterile.

Following these, would greatly minimize the risk of getting affected by diseases.

- Make sure to properly wash your hand before beginning to process your meat. Use fresh tap water and soap/hand sanitizer.
- Make sure to remove any metal ornaments such as rings and watches from your wrist and hand before starting to handle the meat.
- Thoroughly clean the cutting surface using sanitizing liquid to remove any grease or unwanted contaminates. If you want to go for a homemade sanitizer, then you can simply make a solution of 1 part chlorine bleach and 10 parts water.
- The above-mentioned sanitizer should also be used to soak your tools such as knives and other equipment to ensure that they are safe to use as well.
- Alternatively, commercial acid-based/ no rinsed sanitizers such as Star San will also work.
- After each and every use, all of the knives and other equipment such as meat grinders, slicers, extruders, etc. should be cleaned thoroughly using soap water. The knives should be taken care of in particular by cleaning the place just on top of the handle as it might contain blood and pieces of meat.

- When it comes to cleaning the surface, you should use cloths or sponges

Asides from the tips above, two other things that you should keep in mind are:

- You should always make sure that you keep storing your meat in a place where the temperature is lower than 40 degrees Fahrenheit as studies have shown that temperatures of 40-140 degrees Fahrenheit provide the optimal temperature for bacterial growth.
- If you are using pre-packed meat, then there remains a risk that the meat will eventually diminish after you open the package. However, this process can be significantly decelerated with the help of some excellent guidelines to cover your meat. (next section provides the rules)

A simple guideline to cover and wrap your meat

- Using aluminum foil to cover up your meat will help to protect it from light and oxygen and keep the moisture intact. However, since Aluminum is reactive, it is advised that a layer of plastic wrap is used underneath the aluminum foil to provide a double protective layer.
- If keeping the meat in a bowl with no lid, then a plastic wrap can be used to seal the bowl providing an airtight enclosure.
- Re-sealable bags provide protection by storing it in a bag and squeezing out any air.
- Airtight glass or plastic containers with lids are a good option as well.
- A type of paper known as Freezer paper is specifically designed to wrap foods that are to be kept in the fridge. These wraps are amazing for meat as well.
- Vacuum sealers are often used for Sous Vide packaging. These machines are a bit expensive but are able to provide excellent packaging by completely sucking out any air from a re-sealable bag. This greatly increases the meats shelf life both outside and in the fridge.

A Note on Sanitation

Keeping your cooking station clean should always be on the top of your priority list when cooking!

While cooking and experimenting with various ingredients, you will be dealing with different types of blemishes. Try to keep the following cleaners to help you deal with the different types of unnecessary materials:

- **Detergent/Dish Washing Liquid:** These are perfect for removing simple dust and surface oil.
- **Solvent Cleaners/Ammonia:** These contain grease-dissolving agents and help to clean similar materials.
- **Acid Cleaners as Hydrochloric Acid:** These contain grease-dissolving agents and help to clean similar materials.

- **Abrasive Cleaners:** These can clean materials such as fine steel, wool, nylon and copper
- **Solvent Cleaners/Ammonia:** These contain grease-dissolving agents and help to clean similar materials.
- **Sanitizers:** These are really good for cleaning the food preparation surface. These include:
  - ✓ Chlorine Bleach
  - ✓ Hydrogen Peroxide
  - ✓ White distilled vinegar

Tips to Prevent Cross-Contamination

Cross Contamination is one of the main reasons for food-borne diseases to spread! The following tips will help you to prevent such events from happening.
- Always wash your hand thoroughly with warm water. Also, the cutting boards, counters, knives, and other utensils should also be cleaned as instructed in the first section of the chapter.
- Make sure to keep different types of meat in different bowls, dishes, and plates prior to using them.
- When storing the meat in the fridge, make sure to keep the raw meat, seafood, poultry and eggs on the bottom shelf of your fridge and in individual sealed containers.
- Keep your refrigerator shelves cleaned and juices from meat/vegetables might drip on them.
- Always refrain yourself from keeping raw meat/vegetables on the same plate as cooked goods.
- Always make sure to clean your cutting boards and use different cutting boards for different types of foods. Raw meats, vegetables, and other foods should not be cut using the same table.

FAQ
If this if your first time, then it's almost certain that you are going to have some questions regarding Meal Prep.
Let me clear some of the most common ones for you before letting you go into the recipes!
Q1. How long does stored food usually last?
As a rule of thumb, you should not store your food for more than 4 days in airtight containers.
Q2. How should you store meal prepped food?
A good way is to use plastic containers to store cooked food. Make sure to allow your meals to cool for 30-40 minutes before sealing them though.
Q3. What does buffet meal prep mean?

A buffet meal prep is when you batch cook a number of different ingredients and then create meals during the week as you keep on going, instead of prepping all the meals at once.

Q4. What type of containers should you use?

Plastic containers are BPA free, microwave and dishwasher safe so these are really cool to use.

Q5. How should you motivate yourself to meal prep every week?

Good pointers to remember is that meal prep will help you to stay healthy, energy and maintain a very healthy physique! And most importantly, it will help you save up a lot of money.

Q6. Is Freezing good?

While freezing meals are not recommended (as re-heating them sometimes diminishes the flavor), you are more than welcome to chill sauces, soups, chilis, etc. and thaw them when needed.

Q7. How are you to re-heat workweek lunches without ruining them?

When you are in the office, re-heat your meals using the office microwave, and while at home...try to re-heat your meal in oven or stove (it preserves the flavor almost perfectly)

And that pretty much covers the basics of Meal Prep!

Now, let's dig deep into a step by step guide as to how you can actually prepare a healthy meal plan.

Chapter 4: A Quick Meal Prep Guideline And 30 Days Meal Plan

There is a very close relation between Meal Plan and Meal Prepping!

As you may have already assumed, Meal Planning is creating an outline of what you are going to eat for the rest of the week, Meal Prepping would be to focus on that outline and prepare the ingredients of your meals accordingly so that you can prepare them easily over the coming days.

That being said, this particular chapter will focus on showing you a sample meal prep guideline using sample recipes, which should be used as a template when creating your own meal plans!

But don't worry at all, as I have provided a sample meal plan (using recipes from this book) for you as well!

Now don't be nervous at all! With the ideas provided in this book and this sample, you should be able to come up with your own plans in no time!

Step 1: Choosing A Day

The first step of your meal prep regime is to pick a day when you will prepare all of your meals. Weekends are perfect since you will be getting the most time on that day. If you are a family person, then your kids and spouse will be at home as well who might be able to help you to make the whole process faster!

More experienced meal preppers tend to prefer Sunday and Wednesday as their preparing days and divide the total work between these two days.

When beginning though, you should not plan meals for the whole week as it might be too much! Try to prepare three meals at the beginning and keep increasing the number as you become more proficient.

Step 2: Choose your meals

The next step is to choose the meals that you are going to prepare for breakfast, lunch, and dinner.

If you are preparing for the whole family, then dinner meals will be the one where most of your efforts will go.

When choosing the recipes though, you should try to maintain your specific macronutrient goal depending on your guide. (Protein, Fat, and carb are to be considered)

Once you have decided on your meals, the next step is to make a shopping list of the ingredients that you are going to need for the meals.

Step 3: Equipment and Shopping List

So, let's say that we are going to need the following ingredients

- 2.5 pound of chicken meat
- 2 large bags of mixed vegetables such as broccoli, carrots, cauliflower, etc.
- 2 and a ½ pound of sweet potatoes

- Salt and pepper as needed alongside any seasoning mix that you might need

As for the equipment

- 2 baking sheets
- Aluminum foil as needed
- A large-sized pot
- Colander
- Cutting board
- Knife
- Non-stick cooking spray
- Containers such as plastic containers or bags

Keep in mind that all of this equipment has already been discussed in the previous chapter.

Step 4: The Process

Keep in mind that the meal prepping process will largely vary depending on the type of ingredients you are using, for the above sample, the first order of business would be to:

- Take a large-sized pot and dump the vegetables, add water until the veggies are covered and boil the vegetables properly
- While you are boiling your vegetables, pre-heat your oven to 350 degrees Fahrenheit
- Take the baking sheet and cover with aluminum foil, spray with non-stick cooking spray. Transfer the chicken thigh and season with salt and pepper as needed
- Bake them for 25 minutes
- While baking, Wash the potatoes well and cut them very carefully into rounds and slice the rounds into smaller chunks
- Transfer the chunks to another baking sheet and transfer the sheet to your oven, bake for 30 minutes
- By now the veggies should be ready, so take them out and strain them in a colander
- Take five different plastic containers and add the veggies to the container
- If you want, then you may portion them out as needed
- The chicken should be ready now, so take them out and portion them between the containers
- Do the same for the sweet potatoes

And you are done! By the end, you should have something looking like this.

And that was a demo as to how you should prepare your meals.

Once again, keep in mind that the process will vary depending on the recipes that you are using,

Just to make things even clearer, below is a 30 days meal plan made using the recipes found in this book that should further help you to understand the concept.

Keep in mind that the following is just to be taken as a template and you will be able to change it according to your needs.

Since I am aiming this plan at beginners, I will be keeping just 2 recipes for each breakfast, lunch, and dinner per week. This would lower down the variety but would make it easier for you to prepare.

Also, we have taken Sunday and Wednesday as the meal prep days, if you are free on any other day, you may shift them accordingly.

Some things to keep in mind when going into the meal plan are:

- Prepare your shopping list by comparing the individual ingredients require for each of the recipes. If the recipes have similar ingredients such as seasoning, meat or vegetables, combine them and buy the amount in bulk.
- Try to keep the variety of recipes to a minimum at the beginning as it might be difficult for you to prepare so many ingredients at once.
- Have a look at the ideas provided in the previous chapter to prepare your ingredients accordingly and store them in the long run. For example, you may use the technique of freezing your smoothies in muffin tins for the smoothies used in the meal plan

Chapter 5: The Powerful 28 Days Meal Plan

The following meal plan is made using recipes found in this book. Keep in mind that you are allowed to experiment with it and come up with your own plan if you want.

Week 1	Breakfast	Lunch	Dinner
Day 1 (Sunday)	Meal Prep Day	Meal Prep Day	Meal Prep Day
Day 2 (Monday)	Lovely Porridge	Grilled Chicken Platter	Chipotle Lettuce Chicken
Day 3 (Tuesday)	Lovely Porridge	Grilled Chicken Platter	Chipotle Lettuce Chicken
Day 4 (Wednesday)	Yogurt And Kale Smoothie	Mushroom Pork Chops	Classical Medi Pork
Day 5 (Thursday)	Yogurt And Kale Smoothie	Grilled Chicken Platter	Chipotle Lettuce Chicken
Day 6 (Friday)	Basil And Tomato Baked Eggs	Mushroom Pork Chops	Classical Medi Pork
Day 7 (Saturday)	Meal Prep Day	Meal Prep Day	Meal Prep Day

We tried to keep a low variation in the recipe to ensure that things don't get too difficult for you. But as mentioned, don't you can change it in any way you want.

Week 2	Breakfast	Lunch	Dinner
Day 1 (Sunday)	Meal Prep Day	Meal Prep Day	Meal Prep Day
Day 2 (Monday)	Salty Macadamia Chocolate Smoothie	Grilled Chicken Platter	Chipotle Lettuce Chicken
Day 3 (Tuesday)	Cinnamon And Coconut Porridge	Parsley Chicken Breast	Avocado Beef Patties
Day 4 (Wednesday)	Basil And Tomato Baked Eggs	Walnut Salmon	Grilled Lime Shrimp
Day 5 (Thursday)	Lovely Porridge	Mustard Chicken	Mediterranean Tuna Salad
Day 6 (Friday)	Lovely Porridge	Parsley Chicken Breast	Avocado Beef Patties
Day 7 (Saturday)	Meal Prep Day	Meal Prep Day	Meal Prep Day

Week 3	Breakfast	Lunch	Dinner
Day 1 (Sunday)	Meal Prep Day	Meal Prep Day	Meal Prep Day
Day 2 (Monday)	Yogurt And Kale Smoothie	Grilled Chicken Platter	Chipotle Lettuce Chicken
Day 3 (Tuesday)	Spicy Jalapeno Popper Deviled Eggs	Grilled Chicken Platter	Chipotle Lettuce Chicken
Day 4 (Wednesday)	Yogurt And Kale Smoothie	Mushroom Pork Chops	Classical Medi Pork
Day 5 (Thursday)	Spicy Jalapeno Popper Deviled Eggs	Mustard Chicken	Mediterranean Tuna Salad
Day 6 (Friday)	Cinnamon Roll Chiller	Parsley Chicken Breast	Avocado Beef Patties
Day 7 (Saturday)	Meal Prep Day	Meal Prep Day	Meal Prep Day

Week 4	Breakfast	Lunch	Dinner
Day 1 (Sunday)	Meal Prep Day	Meal Prep Day	Meal Prep Day
Day 2 (Monday)	Basil And Tomato Baked Eggs	Herbed Butter Pork Chops	Butter Beans
Day 3 (Tuesday)	Cinnamon And Coconut Porridge	Stuffed Salmon Avocado	Stuffed Mushrooms
Day 4 (Wednesday)	Basil And Tomato Baked Eggs	Herbed Butter Pork Chops	Butter Beans
Day 5 (Thursday)	Cinnamon And Coconut Porridge	Stuffed Salmon Avocado	Stuffed Mushrooms
Day 6 (Friday)	Yogurt And Kale Smoothie	Lovely Turtle Salad	Garlic And Lemon Soup
Day 7 (Saturday)	Meal Prep Day	Meal Prep Day	Meal Prep Day

Chapter 6: A Look Into Various Diabetic-Friendly Diet

One of the best ways to reverse Diabetes is to essentially follow a proper diet. You have no idea just how much a healthy diet can help to turn your life around!

This chapter contains a brief look into some of the top diets that you can look into if you are hoping to reverse your diabetes and slowly return your blood glucose to normal levels.

So, first off, let's start off with DASH.

What is Dash Diet?

The word DASH is an acronym that stands for "Dietary Approaches to Stop Hypertension" and is an extremely healthy way of living the life that significantly helps to lower down blood pressure levels and make you resistant to various diseases.

Why the DASH Diet?

In one word "Salt".

Overexposure of Salt (more than 500mg per day) has the power to silently wreak- havoc inside your body and negatively affect your overall health by increasing your blood pressure, leading to hypertension, which in turn leads to various cardiovascular diseases.

The saddest truth, however, is the fact that despite knowing the side-effects of salt consumption, American foods these days are packed with more salt than ever!

Processed food, Junk foods are running around every corner these days! In order to save time, Americans are leaning more towards these unhealthy Fast Foods as opposed to a hearty homely meal.

The result?

Slowly but surely, Americans are destroying their health in the long run!

In fact, at the time of writing, it was statistically estimated that every one out of three Americans are bound to develop high blood pressure due to increased salt intake.

So yes, the situation is pretty grim. But that does not mean that it is the end though!

In order to tackle this very scenario, the DASH diet was created.

The underlying concept of the DASH diet

There are a good number of different diets out there that each tries to teach various concepts that help to lose excess weight. There's the Ketogenic Diet, Atkins, Paleo...the list goes on.

However, none of the "Weightloss" diets tend to tackle the issues of our high sodium intake.

And this is exactly where the DASH diet stands out from the crowd.

The core objective of the diet is not trimming down your excess fat, rather it tries to improve your overall health in the long run by helping you lower down your blood pressure levels and enhance your immunity against hypertension and various forms of cardiovascular diseases.

What's even more interesting about this diet is the fact that you will start seeing results within just a week or two!

As for the dietary restriction of the DASH diet, you won't have to sacrifice any of your favorite foods from your life!

While the diet does primarily focus on increasing intake of fruits, vegetables, low-fat dairy items, and grains, it doesn't necessarily force you to completely omit meat!

When it comes to meat, its best to avoid red meat such as beef/pork as much as possible and opt for poultry and seafood.

All in all, the key thing to remember is the fact that while on a DASH diet, you are brings your sodium intake under control. Recommended levels are 1500mg per day.

Just to bring this into perspective, a typical American diet consists of more than 3,400mg per day!

Advantages of Dash Diet

That being said, just keeping your blood pressure under control isn't the only thing the DASH diet is good at!

Since you will go on a healthy food spree, the following benefits will also bless you!

- Helps to lower down cholesterol levels
- Helps in weight loss (discussed later)
- Gives you a healthier heart
- Helps to prevent Osteoporosis
- Helps to improve Kidney health
- Helps to prevent cancer
- Helps to control Diabetes
- Helps to prevent depression

And those are just the tip of the iceberg!

Going deep into the dietary requirement

By now you should have a clear idea of the core concepts of the DASH Diet, and you should also understand that the DASH Diet won't necessarily impose a very strict diet regime upon you!

Yet again, the "Key" factor to remember is to lower down your salt.

So, to properly maintain your DASH diet, you are too-

- Consume more fruits, low-fat dairy foods, and vegetables
- Try to cut back on foods that are high in cholesterol, saturated fat and trans fat
- Eat more whole-grain foods, nuts, poultry and fish

- Try to limit down on sodium, sugary drinks, sweets and red meat such as beef/pork, etc.

Researches have shown that you will be getting the result within just 2 weeks! Alternatively, a different form of diet known as DASH-Sodium calls for cutting down sodium to about 1,500 mg per day (which weighs to about 2/3 teaspoon per day)

Generally speaking, the suggested DASH routine includes:

- Daily 7-8 servings of Grains
- Daily 4-5 servings of vegetables
- Daily 4-5 servings of Fruits
- Daily 2-3 servings of Low-Fat/ Fat-Free dairy products
- 2 or less daily servings of Meat/ Fish/ Poultry
- 4-5 servings per week of nuts, dry beans, and seeds
- 2-3 daily servings of Fats and Oil
- Less than 5 servings per week of sweets

And just to give you an idea of what "Each" serving means, here are a few pointers.

The following quantities are to be considered as 1 serving

- ½ a cup of cooked rice/pasta
- 1 sliced of bread
- 1 cup of raw fruit or veggies
- ½ a cup of cooked fruit or veggies
- 8 ounce of milk
- 3 ounce of cooked meat
- 1 teaspoon of olive oil/ or any healthy oil
- 3 ounce of tofu

Cool tips for the future!

The following tips will help you make your DASH diet more effective and bear the positive results more quickly!

- Always make sure to increase the number of fruits and vegetables you consume daily (Fresh/Frozen). You will find plenty of recipes based on vegetables and fruits in this book! However, try to make a habit out of it and try to make up half of your plate with fresh fruits and vegetables.
- When creating a meal plan, make sure to substitute any Red Meat-based recipes with legume-based meals, poultry or fish. This will ensure that you are enjoying the full effect of the DASH diet.
- Try to go for whole-grain products as much as possible! Whole Wheat Bread, oats, pasta, quinoa, brown rice and so on.
- When opting dairy, go for low-fat milk or yogurt and avoid sugary carbonated beverages as much as possible.

- Try to consume a good amount of unsalted nuts and seeds.
- Try to develop a habit of reading nutritional facts on food labels and compare them to find the foods that are made up of the lowest amount of saturated and trans fat.
- Add a serving of veggies at dinner and lunch
- Add a serving of fruit to your meals or such as snacks
- If you wish, then you are allowed to go for low-fat/ skim dairy products as a replacement for full-fat/cream
- If you have a craving for snacks, try to go for unsalted pretzels, raisins or nuts instead of chips or sweets

Now let's have a look at Paleo.

Looking deeply into Paleo "The Caveman Diet"

Whenever we are talking about a Caveman's Diet (Paleo), we are mostly referring to a diet that can bring the right amount of protein, calories, carbs, etc. without overly relying on processed or toxic foods.

Generally speaking, research from Emory University suggests that it is advisable for people who follow a Paleo diet to take 35% of their total calorie intake from fats, the rest of the 35% from carbohydrates and the final 30% from the proteins.

What to expect during early Paleo days

As you can already expect, the Paleo diet will bring about some significant changes to the healthy diet that you are used to.

Years and years of evolution in the way we eat have caused our body to re-orient itself into thinking that these 'processed" foods are the way to go!

So, naturally, when you start to cut back on all of the junks, your body will show some changes.

I want you to understand that experiencing the following symptoms is extraordinarily healthy and there is nothing to afraid of!

- A proper Paleo diet dramatically aids in weight loss, albeit indirectly. The abundance of protein and fat in your body creates satiety which gives you a feeling of being full. The body meets up with the nutritional requirements of your body; as a result, you won't have to eat that much, and as such, the body will start up losing weight.
- The increased intake of amino acids and healthy fats will help you to improve digestion.
- Regarding a physiological change, following a Paleo diet will significantly help your body to gain muscle which is highly essential for individuals who might be suffering from underweight.
- The increased level of libido thanks to a more balanced weight will also affect the level of hormones in your body and balance them out to allow you to control your emotions and sexual drives even better

- Having a Paleo diet will encourage your body to get more essential elements such as Omega 3 Fatty acids, B5, Selenium and even zinc 5 which altogether helps to make your skin much softer and brighter with a reduced chance of acne
- If you are suffering from tooth decay, then a Paleo diet will help to a great length as it will help you to stay away from sugary stuff that might cause damage to your enamel
- Since you are going for more and leafier vegetables, they will help to increase the level of Leptin that will encourage the level of fertility in your body.
- Since you are keeping yourself away from Dairy products and caffeine, if you are a female you will experience lesser cramps during periods

Amazing advantages of following the diet

The Paleo Diet comes with a barrage of fantastic health benefits that you will enjoy in the long run!

To encourage you even further to explore the diet itself and embrace its way of life, here are just some of the crucial ones!

Accelerated Weight Loss

The low-carb clean eating regime of the Paleo diet dramatically helps to turn the body into a fat-burning machine that accelerates the amount of fat burnt through various activates.

This is discussed in greater detail in a section later on.

Improved Intestinal Health

A diet consisting of highly processed foods and chemicals often leads to the stomach and intestinal lining issues and causes leaky gut and other problems. Since the Paleo diet encourages you to let go of all of these harmful food items, you will eventually start to protect the health of your gut and improve it as well.

Right Amount Of Vitamins and Minerals

The traditional Western Diet that we usually tend to follow contains more rubbish and less nutrition! The Paleo diet will help you to bring forth a sense of balance in the food that you consume and provide you with a sufficient amount of minerals and vitamins to keep you healthy.

Eliminates Allergens From Diet

The food list of the Paleo diet is designed in such a way that it greatly helps to reduce allergens such as dairy and grains from the diet, improving your overall tolerance in the long run.

Lowers Inflammation

Paleo Diet encourages an individual to go for food that is rich in Omega-3 fatty acids, and these foods have been shown to reduce inflammation.

The benefit? With reduced inflammation, you will start to experience relief from various autoimmune diseases such as rheumatoid arthritis, bronchitis, sinusitis, asthma, etc.

The Paleo diet has also been seen to improve your cardiovascular health as well!

Gives More Energy
The clean and healthy diet plan will allow your body to have more energy to spend naturally!
Unlike other processed foods, the healthy alternatives will stay in your body for a really long and slowly keep releasing energy over the day.
This allows your body to stay pumped and avoid any feeling of lethargy!
And those were just the tip of the Ice Berg!

The Paleo Food List
With all said and done, you must be wondering about the foods that are allowed on the Paleo diet? Well, to give you a rough summary:

Foods To Eat
- Meats including Lamb, Beef, Turkey, Chicken, Pork
- Seafood such as trout, haddock, shellfish
- Omega-3 enriched eggs
- Lots and lots of vegetables including peppers, kale, broccoli, carrots, onions, etc.
- Fruits as Bananas, Apples, Pears, Strawberries, Avocados and also Blueberries
- Tubers including sweet potatoes, turnips, yams
- Nuts and seeds such as Macadamia, Almonds, Walnuts, Hazelnuts, Sunflower Seeds
- Fats and Oil as Coconut Oil, Avocado Oil, Olive Oil
- Salts such as Himalayan Salt, Seas Salt, Turmeric, Garlic and Rosemary

Foods Not To Eat
- Items that are high in fructose or sugar such as drinks, candy, fruit juices
- Grain type items such as wheat, rye, barley
- Legumes as lentils
- Vegetable oil such as corn oil, sunflower oil, soybean oil
- Hydrogenated products
- Artificial Sweeteners
- Heavily processed foods

And now, let me dive a little bit deeper into the allowed list.

Meat
The following is a list of meat that you seamlessly enjoy while on a Paleo diet. Remember to try to obtain them as fresh as possible and avoid processed meats such as hot dogs, spam, etc.
- Chicken liver
- Pork loin
- Duck

- Goat Meat
- Lean hamburger
- Chuck Steak
- Lean Beef
- Flank Steak
- Lean Chicken Breast
- Pork Chops
- Turkey Breast
- Goose
- Lean Poultry
- Lean Pork, Trimmed
- Top Sirloin Steak
- Lean Veal
- Rabbit Meat
- Organ meats of Chicken, Beef, Pork, and Lamb

Fish and Seafood

Generally, all fish are allowed on a Paleo as they are packed with omega-3 fatty acids.

- Scrod
- Shrimp
- Tuna
- Scallops
- Crab
- Herring
- Flatfish
- Red snapper
- Crayfish
- Lobster
- Monkfish
- Perch
- Halibut
- Mackerel
- Northern pike
- Trout
- Salmon
- Mussels
- Rockfish
- Turbot
- Drum

- Oysters
- shark

Nuts and Seeds

When considering nuts, you should keep in mind that cashews are high in fat and addictive! So try to control your portions. If you are trying to lose weight while on a Paleo diet, maybe you should consider cutting down your nut intake.

- pecans
- almonds
- Hazelnuts
- Walnuts
- Pumpkin seeds
- Sunflower seeds
- Brazil nuts
- Macadamia Nuts
- Pistachios
- Cashews
- Sesame Seeds
- Chestnuts
- Pine Nuts

Veggies

Almost all veggies are allowed on a Paleo diet! However, certain high-starch veggies such as squash and potatoes should be taken in moderation.

- Watercress
- Swiss chard
- Radish
- Turnips
- Asparagus
- Tomato
- Lettuce
- Bell peppers
- Turnip greens
- Kohlrabi
- Spinach
- Dandelion
- Seaweed
- Onions
- Parsnips
- Mustard greens

- Pumpkin
- Cauliflower
- Parsley
- Green onions
- Cabbage
- Mushrooms
- Kale
- Celery
- Mushrooms
- Broccoli
- Eggplant
- Collards
- Brussels sprouts
- Cucumber
- Artichokes
- Carrots
- Yam
- Acorn squash
- Butternut squash
- Beets
- Sweet potatoes

Oils and Fats
- Olive oil
- Coconut oil
- Avocado oil
- Macadamia oil

Fruits

Fruits are pretty delicious and nutritious as well! But at the same time, they have a very high sugar value. Even the Paleo-approved ones contain a hefty dose of fructose. Therefore, if your aim to lose weight, try to keep your fruit intake on a basal level and learn more towards vegetables.

- Avocado
- Apple
- Blackberries
- Plums
- Peaches
- Papaya
- Grapes
- Mango

- Lychee
- Orange
- Lemon
- Lime
- Tangerine
- Cantaloupe
- Raspberries
- Strawberries
- Guava
- Watermelon
- Pineapple
- Bananas
- Figs

Spices and Herbs

- cinnamon
- caraway
- bay leaves
- arise
- basil
- celery seeds
- cayenne pepper
- ginger
- garlic
- chives
- cilantro
- coriander
- clove
- cumin
- curry
- dill
- fenugreek
- Fennel
- Horseradish
- Juniper berry
- Lavender
- Lemongrass
- Rosemary
- Marjoram

- Wasabi
- Mint
- Vanilla
- Turmeric
- Tarragon
- Thyme
- Black Pepper
- Peppermint
- Parsley
- Paprika
- Oregano
- Mustard

And the Foods to avoid

As a general rule of thumb, you should avoid all refined, processed foods alongside sugar, legumes, and grains. For a stricter Paleo regime, you should prevent all dairies as well!

- Milk
- Yogurt
- Butter
- Kefir
- Buttermilk
- Cream
- Cottage Cheese
- Daily Spreads
- Ice Cream
- Soft Drinks
- Fruit Juices (canned)/ you are allowed to have fresh fruit juices from certain fruits such as orange, lemon, lime, pineapple, etc.
- Stay away from all sorts of grains
- Legumes
- Beans including kidney beans, horse beans, fava beans, Garbanzo beans, broad beans, black beans, white beans, red beans, pinto beans, navy beans, mung beans, lima beans, string beans, green beans
- Peas such as sugar snap peas, snow peas, chickpeas, black-eyed peas, lentils, miso, peanuts, peanut butter, soybeans, lupines, tofu, etc.
- All kinds of artificial sweeteners! (use maple syrup/honey to sweeten food)
- Salty/processed foods such as Ketchup, French Fries

Now A look at the Mediterranean.

What is Mediterranean Diet

If you are in the market looking for a diet that will take care of your health and your heart while still being incredibly delicious, the Mediterranean Diet is the way to go!

Generally speaking, the Mediterranean diet is a diet that is built upon a foundation that comprises all the basics of healthy eating and indirectly influences and encourages an individual always to choose essential and healthy ingredients that would improve their overall health.

At its heart, the Mediterranean diet does this by putting a lot of emphasis on going for more and more green foods while replacing dairies such as butter with other healthy oils such as canola or olive oil.

The core of the diet

Going a little deeper into the diet, you will notice that the Mediterranean Diet is named as such because it incorporates the traditional healthy eating and living habits of people from countries that are across the Mediterranean Sea.

The list includes France, Spain, Greece, and Italy.

Depending on which region you are considering, the diet varies a lot, so there is no one "Strict" definition of the Diet.

However, the core of the diet will always remain the same regardless of which region you are considering.

This means, always go for more vegetables, fruit, legumes, nuts, fish, cereals, etc. and unsaturated fats such as olive oil!

It is highly recommended that you keep your dairy and meat intake as low as possible.

That being said, here is a brief list of the core ingredients used by individuals, depending on the regions.

Southern Italy:
- Anchovies
- Balsamic Vinegar
- Basil
- Bay Leaf
- Parsley
- Mozzarella Cheese
- Olive Oil
- Oregano
- Mushrooms
- Rosemary
- Sage
- Thyme
- Tomatoes

Greece:
Basil
- Cucumbers
- Dill
- Feta Cheese
- Fennel
- Honey
- Garlic
- Lemon
- Pepper
- Saffron
- Turmeric

Morocco:
- Cinnamon
- Cumin
- Dried Fruits
- Ginger
- Lemon
- Mint
- Paprika
- Parsley
- Saffron
- Turmeric
- Pepper

Spain:
- Almonds
- Anchovies
- Cheese (Goat, Sheep, and Cow)
- Garlic
- Ham
- Honey
- Onions
- Olive Oil
- Oregano
- Rosemary
- Nuts
- Paprika
- Thyme

The eating habit of the Mediterranean Diet is very closely illustrated in the Mediterranean Food Pyramid as well.

MEATS AND SWEETS
NOT TOO OFTEN
WINE IN MODERATION
POULTRY AND EGGS
DRINK WATER!
CHEESE AND YOGURT
FISH AND SEAFOOD
VEGETABLES, FRUITS, NUTS AND SEEDS GRAINS (MOSTLY WHOLE) OLIVE OIL HERBS AND SPICES
DANCE!
WALK!
EAT MEALS TOGETHER!
PLAY SPORTS!
STAY ACTIVE

As you can see from the diagram above, the Mediterranean Diet is designed following an exceptional balance of foods that are rich in minerals, vitamins, and anti-oxidants.

These are accompanied by a healthy dose of activities that altogether make this diet such a different regime to follow!

The basic outline of the diet

However, if the dietary plan above still feels a bit confusing to you, let me illustrate a brief outline that should help you "ease" into the diet effortlessly.

- Make sure to eat at least 5 portions of a mixed variety of fruits and vegetables every day
- Try to base your meals on starchy food such as potatoes, rice, bread, and pasta. Whenever possible, try to opt for a wholegrain version
- Eat beans, fish, eggs, pulses, meat and other types of protein. Portions of fish and seafood should be higher than meat
- Always make sure to have healthy dairy alternatives and choose the low fat/low sugar versions whenever possible
- Drink about 6-8 glasses of fluid every day
- If you have a meal that is high in salt, fat or sugar, make sure to have them in a small amount

Preparing the Mediterranean Pantry

The following ingredients are the ones that you should keep an eye out for when considering a Mediterranean Diet.

Each of these ingredients is carefully chosen to be compliant with the Mediterranean lifestyle and improve your health in the long run.

- Aleppo Pepper
- Baby Squid
- Bulgur
- Candied Citron
- Cavatelli
- Couscous
- Dried Dates
- Dried Figs
- Golden Raisins
- Pressed Canola Oil
- Feta Cheese
- First, Cold-Pressed, Extra Virgin Olive Oil
- Flax
- Greek Yogurt
- Green Cardamom Pods
- Halloumi Cheese
- Maccheroni
- Manchego
- Medium-Grain Rice
- Medium Grain Spanish Rice
- Orange Blossom Water
- Parmigiano-Reggiano
- Peeled Fava Beans
- Pickling Salt
- Pomegranate Molasses
- Preserved Vine Leaves
- Pure Cinnamon
- Queso Cabrales
- Saffron
- Tahini
- Unfiltered Extra Virgin Olive Oil
- Unrefined Sea Salt
- White Sesame
- Za'atar

To summarize, you should always try to go for

- All kinds of vegetables including tomatoes, kale, broccoli, spinach, cauliflower, Brussels, carrots, cucumbers, etc.
- All types of fruits such as orange, apple, banana, pears, grapes, dates, strawberries, figs, melons, peaches, etc.
- Nuts and seeds such as almonds, Macadamia, walnuts, cashews, sunflower seeds, pumpkin seeds, etc.
- Legumes such as beans, lentils, peas, pulses, chickpeas etc.
- Tubers such as yams, turnips, potatoes, sweet potatoes and so on
- Whole grains such as whole oats, rye, brown rice, corn, barley, buckwheat, whole wheat, whole grain pasta, and bread
- Fish and seafood such as sardines, salmon, tuna, shrimp, mackerel, oyster, crab, clams, mussels, etc.
- Poultry such as turkey, chicken, duck and more
- Eggs including duck, quail and chicken eggs
- Dairy such as cheese, Greek yogurt, etc.
- Herbs and spices such as mint, basil, garlic, rosemary, cinnamon, sage, pepper, etc.
- Healthy fats and oil such as extra virgin olive oil, avocado oil, olives, etc.

And avoid

- Foods with added sugar such as Soda, ice cream, candies, table sugar, etc.
- Refined grains such as white bread or pasta made with refined wheat
- Margarine and similar processed foods that contain Trans Fats
- Refined oil such as cottonseed oil, soybean oil, etc.
- Processed meat such as hot dogs, processed sausages and so on
- Highly processed food with labels such as "Low-Fat" or "Diet" or anything that is not natural

Now, keep in mind that there are many more out there such as Intermittent Fasting, Alkaline and Low Carb that can help you with your diabetes. But the above-mentioned programs are a good place to start. You can always explore more horizons until you find the best one that suits you.

Chapter 7: Breakfast

The Cinnamon Roll Chiller

Serving: 1
Prep Time: 10 minutes
Ingredients:
- 1 cup unsweetened almond milk
- 2 tablespoons vanilla protein powder
- ½ teaspoon cinnamon
- ¼ teaspoon vanilla extract
- 1 tablespoon chia seeds
- 1 cup ice cubs

Directions:
1. Add listed ingredients to a blender
2. Blend until you have a smooth and creamy texture
3. Serve chilled and enjoy!

Nutritional Contents:
- Calories: 145
- Fat: 4g
- Carbohydrates: 1.6g
- Protein: 0.6g

Spicy Jalapeno Popper Deviled Eggs

Serving: 4
Prep Time: 5 minutes
Cook Time: 5 minutes
Ingredients
- 4 large whole eggs, hardboiled
- 2 tablespoons Keto-Friendly mayonnaise
- ¼ cup cheddar cheese, grated
- 2 slices bacon, cooked and crumbled
- 1 jalapeno, sliced

Directions
1. Cut eggs in half, remove the yolk and put them in bowl
2. Lay egg whites on a platter
3. Mix in remaining ingredients and mash them with the egg yolks
4. Transfer yolk mix back to the egg whites

5. Serve and enjoy!

<u>**Nutrition (Per Serving)**</u>

- Calories: 176
- Fat: 14g
- Carbohydrates: 0.7g
- Protein: 10g

Lovely Porridge

Serving: 2
Prep Time: 15 minutes
Cook Time: Nil
<u>**Ingredients**</u>

- 2 tablespoons coconut flour
- 2 tablespoons vanilla protein powder
- 3 tablespoons Golden Flaxseed meal
- 1 and ½ cups almond milk, unsweetened
- Powdered erythritol

<u>**Directions**</u>

1. Take a bowl and mix in flaxseed meal, protein powder, coconut flour and mix well
2. Add mix to the saucepan (placed over medium heat)
3. Add almond milk and stir, let the mixture thicken
4. Add your desired amount of sweetener and serve
5. Enjoy!

<u>**Nutrition (Per Serving)**</u>

- Calories: 259
- Fat: 13g
- Carbohydrates: 5g
- Protein: 16g

Salty Macadamia Chocolate Smoothie

Serving: 1
Prep Time: 5 minutes
Cook Time: Nil
<u>**Ingredients**</u>

- 2 tablespoons macadamia nuts, salted
- 1/3 cup chocolate whey protein powder, low carb
- 1 cup almond milk, unsweetened

Directions
1. Add the listed ingredients to your blender and blend until you have a smooth mixture

2. Chill and enjoy it!

Nutrition (Per Serving)
- Calories: 165
- Fat: 2g
- Carbohydrates: 1g
- Protein: 12g

Basil And Tomato Baked Eggs

Serving: 4
Prep Time: 10 minutes
Cook Time: 15 minutes
Ingredients
- 1 garlic clove, minced
- 1 cup canned tomatoes
- ¼ cup fresh basil leaves, roughly chopped
- ½ teaspoon chili powder
- 1 tablespoon olive oil
- 4 whole eggs
- Salt and pepper to taste

Directions
1. Preheat your oven to 375 degrees F

2. Take a small baking dish and grease with olive oil

3. Add garlic, basil, tomatoes chili, olive oil into a dish and stir

4. Crackdown eggs into a dish, keeping space between the two

5. Sprinkle the whole dish with salt and pepper

6. Place in oven and cook for 12 minutes until eggs are set and tomatoes are bubbling

7. Serve with basil on top

8. Enjoy!

Nutrition (Per Serving)
- Calories: 235
- Fat: 16g
- Carbohydrates: 7g
- Protein: 14g

Cinnamon And Coconut Porridge

Serving: 4
Prep Time: 5 minutes
Cook Time:5 minutes
Ingredients

- 2 cups of water
- 1 cup 36% heavy cream
- ½ cup unsweetened dried coconut, shredded
- 2 tablespoons flaxseed meal
- 1 tablespoon butter
- 1 and ½ teaspoon stevia
- 1 teaspoon cinnamon
- Salt to taste
- Toppings as blueberries

Directions

1. Add the listed ingredients to a small pot, mix well
2. Transfer pot to stove and place it over medium-low heat
3. Bring to mix to a slow boil
4. Stir well and remove the heat
5. Divide the mix into equal servings and let them sit for 10 minutes
6. Top with your desired toppings and enjoy!

Nutrition (Per Serving)

- Calories: 171
- Fat: 16g
- Carbohydrates: 6g
- Protein: 2g

An Omelet Of Swiss Chard

Serving: 4
Prep Time: 5 minutes
Cook Time: 5 minutes
Ingredients

- 4 eggs, lightly beaten
- 4 cups Swiss chard, sliced
- 2 tablespoons butter
- ½ teaspoon garlic salt
- Fresh pepper

How To

1. Take a non-stick frying pan and place it over medium-low heat

2. Once the butter melts, add Swiss chard and stir cook for 2 minutes

3. Pour egg into the pan and gently stir them into Swiss chard

4. Season with garlic salt and pepper

5. Cook for 2 minutes

6. Serve and enjoy!

Nutrition (Per Serving)

- Calories: 260
- Fat: 21g
- Carbohydrates: 4g
- Protein: 14g

Cheesy Low-Carb Omelet

Serving: 5
Prep Time: 5 minutes
Cook Time: 5 minutes
Ingredients

- 2 whole eggs
- 1 tablespoon water
- 1 tablespoon butter
- 3 thin slices salami
- 5 fresh basil leaves
- 5 thin slices, fresh ripe tomatoes
- 2 ounces fresh mozzarella cheese
- Salt and pepper as needed

How To

1. Take a small bowl and whisk in eggs and water

2. Take a non-stick Saute pan and place it over medium heat, add butter and let it melt

3. Pour egg mixture and cook for 30 seconds

4. Spread salami slices on half of egg mix and top with cheese, tomatoes, basil slices

5. Season with salt and pepper according to your taste

6. Cook for 2 minutes and fold the egg with the empty half

7. Cover and cook on LOW for 1 minute

8. Serve and enjoy!

Nutrition (Per Serving)

- Calories: 451

- Fat: 36g
- Carbohydrates: 3g
- Protein:33g

Yogurt And Kale Smoothie

Serving: 1
Prep Time: 10 minutes
Ingredients:
- 1 cup whole milk yogurt
- 1 cup baby kale greens
- 1 pack stevia
- 1 tablespoon MCT oil
- 1 tablespoon sunflower seeds
- 1 cup of water

Directions:
1. Add listed ingredients to the blender
2. Blend until you have a smooth and creamy texture
3. Serve chilled and enjoy!
Nutritional Contents:
- Calories: 329
- Fat: 26g
- Carbohydrates: 15g
- Protein: 11g

Chapter 8: Chicken And Poultry

Bacon And Chicken Garlic Wrap

Serving: 4
Prep Time: 15 minutes
Cook Time: 10 minutes
Ingredients
- 1 chicken fillet, cut into small cubes
- 8-9 thin slices bacon, cut to fit cubes
- 6 garlic cloves, minced

Directions
1. Preheat your oven to 400 degrees F
2. Line a baking tray with aluminum foil
3. Add minced garlic to a bowl and rub each chicken piece with it
4. Wrap bacon piece around each garlic chicken bite
5. Secure with toothpick
6. Transfer bites to the baking sheet, keeping a little bit of space between them
7. Bake for about 15-20 minutes until crispy
8. Serve and enjoy!

Nutrition (Per Serving)
- Calories: 260
- Fat: 19g
- Carbohydrates: 5g
- Protein: 22g

Grilled Chicken Platter

Serving: 6
Prep Time: 5 minutes
Cook Time: 10 minutes
Ingredients
- 3 large chicken breast, sliced half lengthwise
- 10-ounce spinach, frozen and drained
- 3-ounce mozzarella cheese, part-skim
- ½ a cup of roasted red peppers, cut in long strips
- 1 teaspoon of olive oil

- 2 garlic cloves, minced
- Salt and pepper as needed

Directions
1. Preheat your oven to 400 degrees Fahrenheit
2. Slice 3 chicken breast lengthwise
3. Take a non-stick pan and grease with cooking spray
4. Bake for 2-3 minutes each side
5. Take another skillet and cook spinach and garlic in oil for 3 minutes
6. Place chicken on an oven pan and top with spinach, roasted peppers, and mozzarella
7. Bake until the cheese melted
8. Enjoy!

Nutrition(Per Serving)
- Calories: 195
- Fat: 7g
- Net Carbohydrates: 3g
- Protein: 30g

Parsley Chicken Breast

Serving: 4
Prep Time: 10 minutes
Cook Time: 40 minutes
Ingredients
- 1 tablespoon dry parsley
- 1 tablespoon dry basil
- 4 chicken breast halves, boneless and skinless
- ½ teaspoon salt
- ½ teaspoon red pepper flakes, crushed
- 2 tomatoes, sliced

Directions
1. Preheat your oven to 350 degrees F
2. Take a 9x13 inch baking dish and grease it up with cooking spray
3. Sprinkle 1 tablespoon of parsley, 1 teaspoon of basil and spread the mixture over your baking dish
4. Arrange the chicken breast halves over the dish and sprinkle garlic slices on top
5. Take a small bowl and add 1 teaspoon parsley, 1 teaspoon of basil, salt, basil, red pepper and mix well. Pour the mixture over the chicken breast

6. Top with tomato slices and cover, bake for 25 minutes

7. Remove the cover and bake for 15 minutes more

8. Serve and enjoy!

Nutrition (Per Serving)

- Calories: 150
- Fat: 4g
- Carbohydrates: 4g
- Protein: 25g

Mustard Chicken

Serving: 4
Prep Time: 10 minutes
Cook Time: 40 minutes
Ingredients

- 4 chicken breasts
- ½ cup chicken broth
- 3-4 tablespoons mustard
- 3 tablespoons olive oil
- 1 teaspoon paprika
- 1 teaspoon chili powder
- 1 teaspoon garlic powder

Directions

1. Take a small bowl and mix mustard, olive oil, paprika, chicken broth, garlic powder, chicken broth, and chili

2. Add chicken breast and marinate for 30 minutes

3. Take a lined baking sheet and arrange the chicken

4. Bake for 35 minutes at 375 degrees Fahrenheit

5. Serve and enjoy!

Nutrition (Per Serving)

- Calories: 531
- Fat: 23g
- Carbohydrates: 10g
- Protein: 64g

Balsamic Chicken

Serving: 6
Prep Time: 10 minutes
Cook Time: 25 minutes

Ingredients

- 6 chicken breast halves, skinless and boneless
- 1 teaspoon garlic salt
- Ground black pepper
- 2 tablespoons olive oil
- 1 onion, thinly sliced
- 14 and ½ ounces tomatoes, diced
- ½ cup balsamic vinegar
- 1 teaspoon dried basil
- 1 teaspoon dried oregano
- 1 teaspoon dried rosemary
- ½ teaspoon dried thyme

Directions

1. Season both sides of your chicken breasts thoroughly with pepper and garlic salt

2. Take a skillet and place it over medium heat

3. Add some oil and cook your seasoned chicken for 3-4 minutes per side until the breasts are nicely browned

4. Add some onion and cook for another 3-4 minutes until the onions are browned

5. Pour the diced up tomatoes and balsamic vinegar over your chicken and season with some rosemary, basil, thyme, and rosemary

6. Simmer the chicken for about 15 minutes until they are no longer pink

7. Take an instant-read thermometer and check if the internal temperature gives a reading of 165 degrees Fahrenheit

8. If yes, then you are good to go!

Nutrition (Per Serving)

- Calories: 196
- Fat: 7g
- Carbohydrates: 7g
- Protein: 23g

Greek Chicken Breast

Serving: 4
Prep Time: 10 minutes
Cook Time: 25 minutes
Ingredients

- 4 chicken breast halves, skinless and boneless
- 1 cup extra virgin olive oil
- 1 lemon, juiced

- 2 teaspoons garlic, crushed
- 1 and ½ teaspoons black pepper
- 1/3 teaspoon paprika

Directions

1. Cut 3 slits in the chicken breast

2. Take a small bowl and whisk in olive oil, salt, lemon juice, garlic, paprika, pepper and whisk for 30 seconds

3. Place chicken in a large bowl and pour marinade

4. Rub the marinade all over using your hand

5. Refrigerate overnight

6. Pre-heat grill to medium heat and oil the grate

7. Cook chicken in the grill until center is no longer pink

8. Serve and enjoy!

Nutrition (Per Serving)

- Calories: 644
- Fat: 57g
- Carbohydrates: 2g
- Protein: 27g

Chipotle Lettuce Chicken

Serving: 6
Prep Time: 10 minutes
Cook Time: 25 minutes
Ingredients

- 1 pound chicken breast, cut into strips
- Splash of olive oil
- 1 red onion, finely sliced
- 14 ounces tomatoes
- 1 teaspoon chipotle, chopped
- ½ teaspoon cumin
- Pinch of sugar
- Lettuce as needed
- Fresh coriander leaves
- Jalapeno chilies, sliced
- Fresh tomato slices for garnish
- Lime wedges

How To

1. Take a non-stick frying pan and place it over medium heat

2. Add oil and heat it up

3. Add chicken and cook until brown

4. Keep the chicken on the side

5. Add tomatoes, sugar, chipotle, cumin to the same pan and simmer for 25 minutes until you have a nice sauce

6. Add chicken into the sauce and cook for 5 minutes

7. Transfer the mix to another place

8. Use lettuce wraps to take a portion of the mixture and serve with a squeeze of lemon

9. Enjoy!

Nutrition (Per Serving)

- Calories: 332
- Fat: 15g
- Carbohydrates: 13g
- Protein: 34g

Stylish Chicken-Bacon Wrap

Serving: 3
Prep Time: 5 minutes
Cook Time: 50 minutes
Ingredients

- 8 ounces lean chicken breast
- 6 bacon slices
- 3 ounces shredded cheese
- 4 slices ham

How To

1. Cut chicken breast into bite-sized portions

2. Transfer shredded cheese onto ham slices

3. Roll up chicken breast and ham slices in bacon slices

4. Take a skillet and place it over medium heat

5. Add olive oil and brown bacon for a while

6. Remove rolls and transfer to your oven

7. Bake for 45 minutes at 325 degrees F

8. Serve and enjoy!

Nutrition (Per Serving)

- Calories: 275
- Fat: 11g
- Carbohydrates: 0.5g
- Protein: 40g

Chapter 9: Pork

Pork Rinds In A Stick

Serving: 2
Prep Time: 5 minutes
Cook Time: 25 minutes
Ingredients

- 2 medium zucchinis, halved lengthwise and seeded
- ¼ cup crushed pork rinds
- ¼ cup grated parmesan cheese
- 2 garlic cloves, minced
- 2 tablespoons melted butter
- Salt and pepper
- Olive oil for drizzle

Directions

1. Preheat your oven to 400 degrees F

2. Line a baking sheet with aluminum foil

3. Place zucchini halves (cut side facing up) on prepared baking sheet

4. Take a medium bowl and add pork rinds, parmesan cheese, garlic, melted butter, season with pepper and salt

5. Mix well

6. Spoon pork rind mix onto zucchini stick

7. Drizzle olive oil

8. Bake for 20 minutes until the topping is golden brown

9. Turn your broiler and brown for 3-5 minutes

10. Serve and enjoy!

Nutrition (Per Serving)

- Calories: 231
- Fat: 20g
- Carbohydrates: 6g
- Protein: 9g

Mushroom Pork Chops

Serving: 3
Prep Time: 10 minutes
Cook Time: 40 minutes
Ingredients

- 8 ounces mushrooms, sliced
- 1 teaspoon garlic
- 1 onion, peeled and chopped
- 1 cup Keto-Friendly Mayonnaise
- 3 pork chops, boneless
- 1 teaspoon ground nutmeg
- 1 tablespoon balsamic vinegar
- ½ cup of coconut oil

Directions

1. Take a pan and place it over medium heat
2. Add oil and let it heat up
3. Add mushrooms, onions, and stir
4. Cook for 4 minutes
5. Add pork chops, season with nutmeg, garlic powder, and brown both sides
6. Transfer the pan in the oven and bake for 30 minutes at 350 degrees F
7. Transfer pork chops to plates and keep it warm
8. Take a pan and place it over medium heat
9. Add vinegar, mayonnaise over mushroom mix and stir or a few minutes
10. Drizzle sauce over pork chops
11. Enjoy!

Nutrition (Per Serving)

- Calories: 600
- Fat: 10g
- Carbohydrates: 8g
- Protein: 30g

Rib Eyes With Broccoli

Serving: 4
Prep Time: 5 minutes
Cook Time: 15 minutes

Ingredients

- 4 ounces butter
- ¾ pound Ribeye steak, sliced
- 9 ounces broccoli, chopped
- 1 yellow onion, sliced
- 1 tablespoon coconut aminos
- 1 tablespoon pumpkin seeds
- Salt and pepper to taste

Directions

1. Slice steak and the onions
2. Chop broccoli, including the stem parts
3. Take a frying pan and place it over medium heat, add butter and let it melt
4. Add meat and season accordingly with salt and pepper
5. Cook until both sides are browned
6. Transfer meat to a platter
7. Add broccoli and onion to the frying pan, add more butter if needed
8. Brown
9. Add coconut aminos and return the meat
10. Stir and season again
11. Serve with a dollop of butter with a sprinkle of pumpkin seeds
12. Enjoy!

Nutrition (Per Serving)

- Calories: 875
- Fat: 75g
- Carbohydrates: 8g
- Protein: 40g

Herbed Butter Pork Chops

Serving: 3
Prep Time: 5 minutes
Cook Time: 25 minutes
Ingredients

- 1 tablespoon butter, divided
- 2 boneless pork chops
- Salt and pepper to taste
- 1 tablespoon dried Italian seasoning

- 1 tablespoon olive oil

Directions

1. Preheat your oven to 350 degrees F
2. Pat pork chops dry with a paper towel and place them in a baking dish
3. Season with salt, pepper, and Italian seasoning
4. Drizzle olive oil over pork chops
5. Top each chop with ½ tablespoon butter
6. Bake for 25 minutes
7. Transfer pork chops on two plates and top with butter juice
8. Serve and enjoy!

Nutrition (Per Serving)

- Calories: 333
- Fat: 23g
- Carbohydrates: 1g
- Protein: 31g

Mediterranean Pork Dish

Serving: 4
Prep Time: 10 minutes
Cook Time: 35 minutes

Ingredients

- 4 pork chops, bone-in
- Salt and pepper to taste
- 1 teaspoon dried rosemary
- 3 garlic cloves, peeled and minced

Directions

1. Season pork chops with salt and pepper
2. Place in roasting pan
3. Add rosemary, garlic in a pan
4. Preheat your oven to 425 degrees F
5. Bake for 10 minutes
6. Lower heat to 350 degrees F
7. Roast for 25 minutes more
8. Slice pork and divide on plates

9. Drizzle pan juice all over

10. Serve and enjoy!

<u>Nutrition (Per Serving)</u>

- Calories: 165
- Fat: 2g
- Carbohydrates: 2g
- Protein: 26g

Bacon And Blue Cheese Salad

Serving: 2
Prep Time: 15 minutes
Cook Time: 5-7 minutes
<u>Ingredients</u>

- 2 and ½ ounces fresh spinach
- 1 red onion, sliced
- 3-4 tablespoons blue cheese, crumbled
- 2 ounces almond nibs
- 5 ounces bacon strips

<u>Directions</u>

1. Fry bacon for 2-3 minutes each side, cut the bacon and keep it on the side

2. Take your salad plate and place spinach leaves on the bottom

3. Add sliced onion, cheese, bacon

4. Top with almond nibs

5. Use your desired Keto-Friendly salad dressing if needed

6. Toss and enjoy it!

<u>Nutrition (Per Serving)</u>

- Calories: 420
- Fat: 35g
- Carbohydrates: 2g
- Protein: 24g

Onion And Bacon Pork Chops

Serving: 4
Prep Time: 10 minutes
Cook Time: 45 minutes

Ingredients

- 2 onions, peeled and chopped
- 6 bacon slices, chopped
- ½ cup chicken stock
- Salt and pepper to taste
- 4 pork chops

How To

1. Heat up a pan over medium heat and add bacon

2. Stir and cook until crispy

3. Transfer to bowl

4. Return pan to medium heat and add onions, season with salt and pepper

5. Stir and cook for 15 minutes

6. Transfer to the same bowl with bacon

7. Return the pan to heat (medium-high) and add pork chops

8. Season with salt and pepper and brown for 3 minutes

9. Flip and lower heat to medium

10. Cook for 7 minutes more

11. Add stock and stir cook for 2 minutes

12. Return the bacon and onions to the pan and stir cook for 1 minute

13. Serve and enjoy!

Nutrition (Per Serving)

- Calories: 325
- Fat: 18g
- Carbohydrates: 6g
- Protein: 36g

The Classical Medi Pork

Serving: 4
Prep Time: 10 minutes
Cook Time: 35 minutes
Ingredients

- 4 pork chops, bone-in
- Salt and pepper to taste
- 1 teaspoon dried rosemary
- 3 garlic cloves, peeled and minced

How To

1. Season pork chops with salt and pepper
2. Place in roasting pan
3. Add rosemary, garlic in a pan
4. Preheat your oven to 425 degrees F
5. Bake for 10 minutes
6. Lower heat to 350 degrees F
7. Roast for 25 minutes more
8. Slice pork and divide on plates
9. Drizzle pan juice all over
10. Serve and enjoy!

Nutrition (Per Serving)

- Calories: 165
- Fat: 2g
- Carbohydrates: 2g
- Protein: 26g

Chapter 10: Beef

Avocado Beef Patties

Serving: 2
Prep Time: 15 minutes
Cook Time: 10 minutes
Ingredients
- 1 pound of 85% lean ground beef
- 1 small avocado, pitted and peeled
- 2 slices of yellow cheddar cheese
- Salt as needed
- Fresh ground black pepper as needed

Directions
1. Pre-heat and prepare your broiler to high
2. Divide beef into two equal-sized patties
3. Season the patties with salt and pepper accordingly
4. Broil the patties for 5 minutes per side
5. Transfer the patties to a platter and add cheese
6. Slice avocado into strips and place them on top of the patties
7. Serve and enjoy!

Nutrition(Per Serving)
- Calories: 568
- Fat: 43g
- Net Carbohydrates: 9g
- Protein: 38g

Cabbage And Fried Beef

Serving: 4
Prep Time: 5 minutes
Cook Time: 15 minutes
Ingredients
- 1 pound beef, ground
- ½ pound bacon
- 1 onion
- 1 garlic cloves, minced
- ½ head cabbage
- Salt and pepper to taste

Directions

1. Take a skillet and place it over medium heat
2. Add chopped bacon, beef and onion until slightly browned
3. Transfer to a bowl and keep it covered
4. Add minced garlic and cabbage to the skillet and cook until slightly browned
5. Return the ground beef mixture to the skillet and simmer for 3-5 minutes over low heat
6. Serve and enjoy!

Nutrition (Per Serving)

- Calories: 360
- Fat: 22g
- Net Carbohydrates: 5g
- Protein: 34g

Beef Casserole

Serving: 6
Prep Time: 10 minutes
Cook Time: 35 minutes
Ingredients

- 2 teaspoons onion flakes
- 1 tablespoon gluten-free Worcestershire sauce
- 2 pounds ground beef
- 2 garlic clove, peeled and minced
- Salt and pepper to taste
- 1 cup mozzarella cheese, shredded
- 2 cups cheddar cheese, shredded
- 1 cup Russian dressing
- 2 tablespoons sesame seeds, toasted
- 20 dill pickle slices
- 1 romaine lettuce head, torn

Directions

1. Take a pan and place it over medium heat
2. Add beef, onion flakes, Worcestershire sauce, salt, pepper, and garlic
3. Stir for 5 minutes
4. Transfer to a baking dish and add a 1 cup of cheddar, mozzarella cheese, half of the dressing
5. Stir and spread evenly
6. Arrange pickle slices on top

7. Sprinkle remaining cheddar and sesame seeds
8. Transfer to oven and bake for 20 minutes at 350 degrees F
9. Turn oven to broil and broil for 5 minutes
10. Divide lettuce between serving platters and top with remaining dressing
11. Enjoy!

Nutrition (Per Serving)
- Calories: 554
- Fat: 51g
- Carbohydrates: 5g
- Protein: 45g

Awesome Ground Bell Pepper

Serving: 3
Prep Time: 10 minutes
Cook Time: 10 minutes
Ingredients
- 1 onion, chopped
- 2 tablespoons coconut oil
- 1 pound ground beef
- 1 red bell pepper, diced
- 2 cups spinach, chopped
- Salt and pepper to taste

Directions
1. Take a skillet and place it over medium heat
2. Add onion and cook on until slightly browned
3. Add spinach and ground beef
4. Stir fry until done
5. Take the mixture and fill up the bell peppers
6. Serve and enjoy!

Nutrition (Per Serving)
- Calories: 350
- Fat: 23g
- Carbohydrates: 4g
- Protein: 28g

Tamari Steak Salad

Serving: 4
Prep Time: 15 minutes
Cook Time: 10 minutes
Ingredients

- 2 large bunches salad greens
- 8-9 ounces beef steak
- ½ red bell pepper, sliced
- 6-8 cherry tomatoes, cut into halves
- 4 radishes, sliced
- 4 tablespoons olive oil
- ½ tablespoon fresh lemon juice
- 2 ounces gluten-free tamari sauce
- Salt as needed

Directions

1. Marinate steak in tamari sauce
2. Make the salad by adding bell pepper, tomatoes, radishes, salad green, oil, salt and lemon juice to a bowl, and toss them well
3. Grill the steak to your desired doneness and transfer steak on top of the salad platter
4. Let it sit for 1 minute and cut it crosswise
5. Serve and enjoy!

Nutrition (Per Serving)

- Calories: 500
- Fat: 37g
- Carbohydrates: 4g
- Protein: 33g

Zucchini Beef Saute And Coriander Greens

Serving: 4
Prep Time: 10 minutes
Cook Time: 10 minutes
Ingredients

- 10 ounces beef, sliced into 1-2 inch strips
- 1 zucchini, cut into 2-inch strips
- ¼ cup parsley, chopped
- 3 garlic cloves, minced
- 2 tablespoons tamari sauce

- 4 tablespoons avocado oil

Directions

1. Add 2 tablespoons avocado oil in a frying pan over high heat

2. Place strips of beef and brown for a few minutes on high heat

3. Once the meat is brown, add zucchini strips and Saute until tender

4. Once tender, add tamari sauce, garlic, parsley and let them sit for a few minutes more

5. Serve immediately and enjoy!

Nutrition (Per Serving)

- Calories: 500
- Fat: 40g
- Carbohydrates: 5g
- Protein: 31g

Chapter 11: Vegetarian

Butter Beans

Serving: 4
Prep Time: 5 minutes
Cook Time: 12 minutes
Ingredients
- 2 garlic cloves, minced
- Red pepper flakes to taste
- Salt to taste
- 2 tablespoons clarified butter
- 4 cups green beans, trimmed

Directions
1. Bring a pot of salted water to boil
2. Once the water starts to boil, add beans and cook for 3 minutes
3. Take a bowl of ice water and drain beans, plunge them in the ice water
4. Once cooled, keep them on the side
5. Take a medium skillet and place it over medium heat, add ghee and melt
6. Add red pepper, salt, garlic
7. Cook for 1 minute
8. Add beans and toss until coated well, cook for 3 minutes
9. Serve and enjoy!

Nutrition (Per Serving)
- Calories: 93
- Fat: 8g
- Carbohydrates: 4g
- Protein: 2g

Walnuts And Asparagus

Serving: 4
Prep Time: 5 minutes
Cook Time: 5 minutes
Ingredients
- 1 and ½ tablespoons olive oil
- ¾ pound asparagus, trimmed
- ¼ cup walnuts, chopped
- Salt and pepper to taste

Directions

1. Place a skillet over medium heat add olive oil and let it heat up
2. Add asparagus, Saute for 5 minutes until browned
3. Season with salt and pepper
4. Remove heat
5. Add walnuts and toss
6. Serve warm!

Nutrition (Per Serving)

- Calories: 124
- Fat: 12g
- Carbohydrates: 2g
- Protein: 3g

Roasted Cauliflower

Serving: 8
Prep Time: 5 minutes
Cook Time: 30 minutes

Ingredients

- 1 large cauliflower head
- 2 tablespoons melted coconut oil
- 2 tablespoons fresh thyme
- 1 teaspoon Celtic sea salt
- 1 teaspoon fresh ground pepper
- 1 head roasted garlic
- 8 ounces burrata cheese, for garnish
- 2 tablespoons fresh thyme for garnish

Directions

1. Preheat your oven to 425 degrees F
2. Rinse cauliflower and trim, core and sliced
3. Lay cauliflower evenly on a rimmed baking tray
4. Drizzle coconut oil evenly over cauliflower, sprinkle thyme leaves
5. Season with a pinch of salt and pepper
6. Squeeze roasted garlic
7. Roast cauliflower until slightly caramelize for about 30 minutes, making sure to turn once
8. Garnish with fresh thyme leaves and burrata
9. Enjoy!

Nutrition (Per Serving)

- Calories: 129
- Fat: 11g

- Carbohydrates: 6g
- Protein: 7g

Tomato And Basil Soup

Serving: 4
Prep Time: 10 minutes
Cook Time: 15 minutes
Ingredients
- 14.5 ounces tomatoes, diced
- 2 ounces cream cheese
- ¼ cup heavy whipping cream
- ¼ cup basil, fresh and chopped
- 4 tablespoons butter

Directions
1. Add tomatoes into a blender, alongside juices and puree until smooth
2. Take a saucepan and place it over medium heat, add tomato puree, heavy cream, butter, cream cheese and cook for 10 minutes
3. Add basil, season as desired and cook for 5 minutes more
4. Use an immersion blender to blend the mixture
5. Serve and enjoy!
Nutrition (Per Serving)
- Calories: 239
- Fat: 22g
- Carbohydrates: 7g
- Protein: 3g

Garlic And Lemon Soup

Serving: 3
Prep Time: 10 minutes
Cook Time: nil
Ingredients
- 1 avocado, pitted and chopped
- 1 cucumber, chopped
- 2 bunches spinach
- 1 and ½ cups watermelon, chopped
- 1 bunch cilantro, roughly chopped

- Juice from 2 lemons
- ½ cup coconut aminos
- ½ cup lime juice

Directions

1. Add cucumber, avocado to your blender and pulse well
2. Add cilantro, spinach, and watermelon and blend
3. Add lemon, lime juice, and coconut amino
4. Pulse few more times
5. Transfer to a soup bowl and enjoy it!

Nutrition (Per Serving)

- Calories: 100
- Fat: 7g
- Carbohydrates: 6g
- Protein: 3g

Cool Brussels Platter

Serving: 2
Prep Time: 5 minutes
Cook Time: 10-15 minutes
Ingredients

- ¼ cup parmesan cheese, grated
- ¼ cup hazelnuts, whole and skinless
- 1 tablespoon olive oil
- 1 pound Brussels sprouts
- Salt to taste

Directions

1. Pre-heat your oven 350 degrees F
2. Line a baking sheet with parchment paper and trim bottom of Brussels
3. Put leaves in a medium-sized bowl, making sure that they are broken
4. Toss leaves with olive oil and season with salt
5. Spread leaves on baking sheet
6. Roast for 10-15 minutes until crispy
7. Divide between bowls and toss with remaining ingredients
8. Serve and enjoy!

Nutrition (Per Serving)

- Calories: 287
- Fat: 19g
- Carbohydrates: 13g
- Protein: 14g

Generous Fiery Tomato Salad

Serving: 4
Prep Time: 10 minutes
Cook Time: 25 minutes
Ingredients

- ½ cup scallions, chopped
- 1 pound cherry tomatoes
- 3 teaspoons olive oil
- Sea salt and freshly ground black pepper, to taste
- 1 tablespoon red wine vinegar

How To

1. Season tomatoes with spices and oil
2. Heat your oven to 450 degrees Fahrenheit
3. Take a baking sheet and spread the tomatoes
4. Bake for 15 minutes
5. Stir and turn the tomatoes
6. Then again, bake for 10 minutes
7. Take a bowl and mix the roasted tomatoes with all the remaining ingredients
8. Serve and enjoy!

Nutrition (Per Serving)

- Calories: 115
- Fat: 10.4g
- Carbohydrates: 5.4g
- Protein: 12g

Lovely Turtle Salad

Serving: 2
Prep Time: 10 minutes
Cook Time: Nil

Ingredients

- 12 cups of romaine lettuce, chopped
- 1/3 cup of extra virgin olive oil
- 1/3 cup of freshly grated parmesan cheese
- 3 tablespoon of freshly squeezed lemon juice
- 1 and a ½ tablespoon of mayonnaise (Keto-Friendly)
- 1/3 teaspoon of garlic powder

- Freshly ground black pepper

How To
1. Take a pan and place it over medium-low heat
2. Add all of the ingredients and stir them until fully combined
3. Cook for about 5-10 minutes, making sure that the lid is on
4. Remove the lid and keep cooking until any excess liquid goes away
5. Once the rice is soft and creamy, enjoy it!

Nutrition (Per Serving)
- Calories: 93
- Fat: 7g
- Carbohydrates: 4g
- Protein: 3g

Juicy Ground Beef Casserole

Serving: 6
Prep Time: 10 minutes
Cook Time: 35 minutes
Ingredients
- 2 teaspoons onion flakes
- 1 tablespoon gluten-free Worcestershire sauce
- 2 pounds ground beef
- 2 garlic clove, peeled and minced
- Salt and pepper to taste
- 1 cup mozzarella cheese, shredded
- 2 cups cheddar cheese, shredded
- 1 cup Russian dressing
- 2 tablespoons sesame seeds, toasted
- 20 dill pickle slices
- 1 romaine lettuce head, torn

How To
1. Take a pan and place it over medium heat
2. Add beef, onion flakes, Worcestershire sauce, salt, pepper, and garlic
3. Stir for 5 minutes
4. Transfer to a baking dish and add a 1 cup of cheddar, mozzarella cheese, half of the dressing
5. Stir and spread evenly
6. Arrange pickle slices on top
7. Sprinkle remaining cheddar and sesame seeds
8. Transfer to oven and bake for 20 minutes at 350 degrees F

9. Turn oven to broil and broil for 5 minutes

10. Divide lettuce between serving platters and top with remaining dressing

11. Enjoy!

Nutrition (Per Serving)

- Calories: 554
- Fat: 51g
- Carbohydrates: 5g
- Protein: 45g

Majestic Beef And Tomato Squash

Serving: 4
Prep Time: 10 minutes
Cook Time: 60 minutes
Ingredients

- 2 pounds acorn squash, pricked with a fork
- Salt and pepper to taste
- 3 garlic cloves, peeled and minced
- 1 onion, peeled and chopped
- 1 portobello mushroom, sliced
- 28 ounces canned tomatoes, diced
- 1 teaspoon dried oregano
- ¼ teaspoon cayenne pepper
- ½ teaspoon dried thyme
- 1 pound ground beef
- 1 green bell pepper, seeded and chopped

How To

1. Preheat your oven to 400 degrees F

2. Take acorn squash and transfer to the lined baking sheet, bake for 40 minutes

3. Cut in half and let it cool

4. Deseed them

5. Take a pan and place it over medium-high heat, add meat, garlic, onion, and mushroom, stir cook until brown

6. Add salt, pepper, thyme, oregano, cayenne, tomatoes, green pepper, and stir

7. Cook for 10 minutes

8. Stuff squash halves with beef mix

9. Transfer to oven and bake for 10 minutes more

10. Serve and enjoy!

Nutrition (Per Serving)

- Calories: 260
- Fat: 7g
- Carbohydrates: 4g
- Protein: 10g

Chapter 12: Fish And Seafood

Walnut Salmon

Serving: 6
Prep Time: 10 minutes
Cook Time: 14 minutes
Ingredients
- ½ cup walnuts
- 2 tablespoons stevia
- ½ tablespoon Dijon mustard
- ¼ teaspoon dill
- 2 Salmon fillets (3 ounces each)
- 1 tablespoon olive oil
- Salt and pepper to taste

Directions
1. Preheat your oven to 350 degrees F
2. Add walnuts, mustard, stevia to a food processor and process until your desired consistency is achieved
3. Take a frying pan and place it over medium heat
4. Add oil and let it heat up
5. Add salmon and sear for 3 minutes
6. Add walnut mix and coat well
7. Transfer coated salmon to the baking sheet, bake in the oven for 8 minutes
8. Serve and enjoy!

Nutrition (Per Serving)
- Calories: 373
- Fat: 43g
- Carbohydrates: 4g
- Protein: 20g

Glazed Salmon

Serving: 4
Prep Time: 45 minutes
Cook Time: 10 minutes
Ingredients
- 4 pieces salmon fillets, 5 ounces each
- 4 tablespoons coconut aminos
- 4 teaspoon olive oil

- 2 teaspoon ginger, minced
- 4 teaspoon garlic, minced
- 2 tablespoon sugar-free ketchup
- 4 tablespoons dry white wine
- 2 tablespoons red boat fish sauce

Directions

1. Take a bowl and mix in coconut aminos, garlic, ginger, fish sauce, and mix
2. Add salmon and let it marinate for 15-20 minutes
3. Take a skillet/pan and place it over medium heat
4. Add oil and let it heat up
5. Add salmon fillets and cook on HIGH for 3-4 minutes per side
6. Remove dish once crispy
7. Add sauce and wine
8. Simmer for 5 minutes on low heat
9. Return salmon to the glaze and flip until both sides are glazed
10. Serve and enjoy!

Nutrition (Per Serving)

- Calories: 372
- Fat: 24g
- Carbohydrates: 3g
- Protein: 35g

Garlic Butter Shrimp

Serving: 4
Prep Time: 15 minutes
Cook Time: 30 minutes
Ingredients

- 4 pounds shrimp
- 1-2 tablespoons garlic, minced
- ½ cup butter
- 1 tablespoon lemon pepper seasoning
- ½ teaspoon garlic powder

Directions

1. Preheat your oven to 300 degrees F
2. Take a bowl and mix in garlic and butter
3. Place shrimp in a pan and dot with butter garlic mix
4. Sprinkle garlic powder and lemon pepper
5. Bake for 30 minutes
6. Enjoy!

Nutrition (Per Serving)

- Calories: 749
- Fat: 30g
- Net Carbohydrates: 7g
- Protein: 74g

Stuffed Salmon Avocado

Serving: 2
Prep Time: 10 minutes
Cook Time: 30 minutes
Ingredients

- 1 ripe organic avocado
- 2 ounces wild-caught smoked salmon
- 1-ounce fresh goat cheese
- 2 tablespoons extra virgin olive oil
- Salt as needed

Directions

1. Cut avocado in half and deseed

2. Add rest of the ingredients to a food processor and process until coarsely chopped

3. Place mixture into avocado

4. Serve and enjoy!

Nutrition (Per Serving)

- Calories: 525
- Fat: 48g
- Carbohydrates: 4g
- Protein: 19g

Coconut Haddock

Serving: 3
Prep Time: 10 minutes
Cook Time: 12 minutes
Ingredients

- 4 haddock fillets, 5 ounces each, boneless
- 2 tablespoons coconut oil, melted
- 1 cup coconut, shredded and unsweetened
- ¼ cup hazelnuts, ground

- Salt to taste

Directions

1. Preheat your oven to 400 degrees F
2. Line a baking sheet with parchment paper
3. Keep it on the side
4. Pat fish fillets with a paper towel and season with salt
5. Take a bowl and stir in hazelnuts and shredded coconut
6. Drag fish fillets through the coconut mix until both sides are coated well
7. Transfer to a baking dish
8. Brush with coconut oil
9. Bake for about 12 minutes until flaky
10. Serve and enjoy!

Nutrition (Per Serving)

- Calories: 299
- Fat: 24g
- Carbohydrates: 1g
- Protein: 20g

Grilled Lime Shrimp

Serving: 8
Prep Time: 25 minutes
Cook Time: 5 minutes

Ingredients

- 1 pound medium shrimp, peeled and deveined
- 1 lime, juiced
- ½ cup olive oil
- 3 tablespoons Cajun seasoning

Directions

1. Take a re-sealable zip bag and add lime juice, Cajun seasoning, olive oil
2. Add shrimp and shake it well, let it marinate for 20 minutes
3. Preheat your outdoor grill to medium heat
4. Lightly grease the grate
5. Remove shrimp from marinade and cook for 2 minutes per side
6. Serve and enjoy!

Nutrition (Per Serving)

- Calories: 188
- Fat: 3g
- Net Carbohydrates: 1.2g
- Protein: 13g

Simple Sautéed Garlic And Parsley Scallops

Serving: 4
Prep Time: 5 minutes
Cook Time: 25 minutes
Ingredients
- 8 tablespoons butter
- 2 garlic cloves, minced
- 16 large sea scallops
- Salt and pepper to taste
- 1 and ½ tablespoons olive oil

How To
1. Seasons scallops with salt and pepper
2. Take a skillet and place it over medium heat, add oil and let it heat up
3. Saute scallops for 2 minutes per side, repeat until all Scallops are cooked
4. Add butter to the skillet and let it melt
5. Stir in garlic and cook for 15 minutes
6. Return scallops to skillet and stir to coat
7. Serve and enjoy!

Nutrition (Per Serving)
- Calories: 417
- Fat: 31g
- Net Carbohydrates: 5g
- Protein: 29g

A Broccoli And Tilapia Dish To Die For!

Serving: 1
Prep Time: 4 minutes
Cook Time: 14 minutes

Ingredients
- 6 ounce of tilapia, frozen
- 1 tablespoon of butter
- 1 tablespoon of garlic, minced
- 1 teaspoon of lemon pepper seasoning
- 1 cup of broccoli florets, fresh

How To
1. Preheat your oven to 350 degrees Fahrenheit

2. Add fish in aluminum foil packets
3. Arrange broccoli around fish
4. Sprinkle lemon pepper on top
5. Close the packets and seal
6. Bake for 14 minutes
7. Take a bowl and add garlic and butter, mix well and keep the mixture on the side
8. Remove the packet from oven and transfer to a platter
9. Place butter on top of the fish and broccoli, serve and enjoy!

Nutrition (Per Serving)

- Calories: 362
- Fat: 25g
- Net Carbohydrates: 2g
- Protein: 29g

Chapter 13: Snacks And Appetizers

Cashew And Almond Butter

Serving: 1 and ½ cups
Prep Time: 5 minutes
Cook Time: Nil
Ingredients
- 1 cup almonds, blanched
- 1/3 cup cashew nuts
- 2 tablespoons coconut oil
- Salt as needed
- ½ teaspoon cinnamon

Directions
1. Preheat your oven to 350 degrees F
2. Bake almonds and cashews for 12 minutes
3. Let them cool
4. Transfer to a food processor and add remaining ingredients
5. Add oil and keep blending until smooth
6. Serve and enjoy!

Nutrition (Per Serving)
- Calories: 205
- Fat: 19g
- Carbohydrates: 2g
- Protein: 2.8g

Stuffed Mushrooms

Serving: 4
Prep Time: 10 minutes
Cook Time: 15 minutes
Ingredients
- 4 Portobello mushroom
- 1 cup crumbled blue cheese
- 2 teaspoons extra virgin olive oil
- Salt, to taste
- Fresh thyme

Directions
1. Preheat your oven to 350 degrees Fahrenheit

2. Put out the stems from the mushrooms
3. Chop them into small pieces
4. Take a bowl and mix stem pieces with thyme, salt, and blue cheese and mix well
5. Fill up mushroom with the prepared cheese
6. Top them with some oil
7. Take a baking sheet and place the mushrooms
8. Bake for 15 minutes to 20 minutes
9. Serve warm and enjoy!

Nutrition (Per Serving)

- Calories: 124
- Fat: 22.4g
- Carbohydrates: 5.4g
- Protein: 1.2g

Almond Crunchies

Serving: 20 Crackers
Prep Time: 15 minutes
Cook Time: 60 minutes
Ingredients

- ½ cup ground flax seeds
- ½ cup almond flour
- 1 tablespoon coconut flour
- 2 tablespoons shelled hemp seeds
- ¼ teaspoon sea salt, plus more to sprinkle on top
- 1 egg white
- 2 tablespoons unsalted butter, melted

Directions

1. Preheat your oven to 300 degrees F
2. Take a baking sheet and line it with parchment paper, keep the prepared sheet on the side
3. Add flax, coconut flour, almond, salt, hemp seed to a bowl and mix well
4. Add egg and melted butter, mix well
5. Transfer dough to a sheet of parchment paper and cover with another sheet of paper
6. Roll out dough
7. Cut into crackers and bake for 60 minutes
8. Cool and serve!

Nutrition (Per Serving)

- Calories: 47
- Fat: 6g
- Carbohydrates: 1.2g
- Protein: 02g

Roast Herb Crackers

Serving: 75 Crackers
Prep Time: 10 minutes
Cook Time: 120 minutes
Ingredients

- ¼ cup avocado oil
- 10 celery sticks
- 1 sprig fresh rosemary, stem discarded
- 2 sprigs fresh thyme, stems discarded
- 2 tablespoons apple cider vinegar
- 1 teaspoon Himalayan salt
- 3 cups ground flax seeds

Directions

1. Preheat your oven to 225 degrees F
2. Line a baking sheet with parchment paper and keep it on the side
3. Add oil, herbs, celery, vinegar, salt to a food processor and pulse until you have an even mixture
4. Add flax and puree
5. Let it sit for 2-3 minutes
6. Transfer batter to your prepared baking sheet and spread evenly, cut into cracker shapes
7. Bake for 60 minutes, flip and bake for 60 minutes more
8. Enjoy!

Nutrition (Per Serving)

- Calories: 34
- Fat: 5g
- Carbohydrates: 1g
- Protein: 1.3g

Eggplant Fries

Serving: 8
Prep Time: 10 minutes
Cook Time: 15 minutes
Ingredients
- 2 eggs
- 2 cups almond flour
- 2 tablespoons coconut oil, spray
- 2 eggplant, peeled and cut thinly
- Salt and pepper

Directions
1. Preheat your oven to 400 degrees Fahrenheit
2. Take a bowl and mix with salt and black pepper in it
3. Take another bowl and beat eggs until frothy
4. Dip the eggplant pieces into eggs
5. Then coat them with flour mixture
6. Add another layer of flour and egg
7. Then, take a baking sheet and grease with coconut oil on top
8. Bake for about 15 minutes
9. Serve and enjoy!

Nutrition (Per Serving)
- Calories: 212
- Fat: 15.8g
- Carbohydrates: 12.1g
- Protein: 8.6g

Parmesan Crispies

Serving: 8
Prep Time: 5 minutes
Cook Time: 25 minutes
Ingredients
- 1 teaspoon butter
- 8 ounces parmesan cheese, full fat and shredded

Directions
1. Preheat your oven to 400 degrees F
2. Put parchment paper on a baking sheet and grease with butter
3. Spoon parmesan into 8 mounds, spreading them apart evenly
4. Flatten them

5. Bake for 5 minutes until browned

6. Let them cool

7. Serve and enjoy!

Nutrition (Per Serving)

- Calories: 133
- Fat: 11g
- Carbohydrates: 1g
- Protein: 11g

Spicy Chili Crackers

Serving: 30 crackers
Prep Time: 15 minutes
Cook Time: 60 minutes
Ingredients

- ¾ cup almond flour
- ¼ cup coconut four
- ¼ cup coconut flour
- ½ teaspoon paprika
- ½ teaspoon cumin
- 1 and ½ teaspoons chili pepper spice
- 1 teaspoon onion powder
- ½ teaspoon salt
- 1 whole egg
- ¼ cup unsalted butter

How To

1. Preheat your oven to 350 degrees F
2. Take a baking sheet and line it up with parchment paper, keep it on the side
3. Add listed ingredients to food processor and process until you have a nice and firm dough
4. Divide dough into two equal parts
5. Place one ball on a sheet of parchment paper and cover it with another paper
6. Roll it out
7. Cut into crackers and do the same with the other ball
8. Transfer dough to your prepared baking dish and bake for 8-10 minutes
9. Remove from oven and serve
10. Enjoy!

Nutrition (Per Serving)

- Calories: 49
- Fat: 4.1g
- Carbohydrates: 3g
- Protein: 1.6g

Salt And Rosemary Cracker

Serving: 36 Crackers
Prep Time: 10 minutes
Cook Time: 10-15 minutes

Ingredients

- 1 and ½ cups almond flour
- ½ teaspoon Celtic salt
- 1 egg, at room temp
- 2 tablespoons coconut oil
- ¼ teaspoon pepper
- 1 tablespoon rosemary, chopped

How To

1. Pre-heat oven to 350 degrees F
2. Take a baking tray and line it with parchment paper
3. Take a bowl and add almond flour, salt and keep it on the side
4. Take another bowl and add coconut oil, pepper, rosemary
5. Add almond mixture to the bowl
6. Mix well until you have an even dough
7. Transfer dough to a piece of parchment paper, cover with another parchment paper piece and roll it out into a thin layer
8. Cut into crackers, arrange them on prepped baking sheet
9. Bake for 10-15 minutes
10. Let them cool
11. Serve and enjoy!

Nutrition (Per Serving)

- Calories: 66
- Fat: 6g
- Carbohydrates: 1.4g
- Protein: 3g

Chapter 14: Dessert

Tasty Chia And Blackberry Pudding

Serving: 2
Prep Time: 45 minutes
Cook Time: Nil
Ingredients
- ¼ cup chia seeds
- ½ cup blackberries, fresh
- 1 teaspoon liquid sweetener
- 1 cup coconut milk, full fat and unsweetened
- 1 teaspoon vanilla extract

Directions
1. Take the vanilla, liquid sweetener and coconut milk and add to blender
2. Process until thick
3. Add in blackberries and process until smooth
4. Divide the mixture between cups and chill for 30 minutes
5. Serve and enjoy!

Nutrition (Per Serving)
- Calories: 437
- Fat: 38g
- Carbohydrates: 8g
- Protein: 8g

The Heartthrob Lemon Mousse

Serving: 4
Prep Time: 10 + chill time
Cook Time: 10 minutes

Ingredients
- 1 cup coconut cream
- 8 ounces cream cheese, soft
- ¼ cup fresh lemon juice
- 3 pinches salt
- 1 teaspoon lemon liquid stevia

How To
1. Preheat your oven to 350 degrees F

2. Grease a ramekin with butter

3. Beat cream, cream cheese, fresh lemon juice, salt and lemon liquid stevia in a mixer

4. Pour batter into ramekin

5. Bake for 10 minutes then transfer the mouse to serving the glass

6. Let it chill for 2 hours and serve

7. Enjoy!

Nutrition (Per Serving)

- Calories: 395
- Fat: 31g
- Carbohydrates: 3g
- Protein: 5g

Spicy Popper Mug Cake

Serving: 2
Prep Time: 5 minutes
Cook Time: 5 minutes
Ingredients

- 2 tablespoons almond flour
- 1 tablespoon flaxseed meal
- 1 tablespoon butter
- 1 tablespoon cream cheese
- 1 large egg
- 1 bacon, cooked and sliced
- ½ a jalapeno pepper
- ½ teaspoon baking powder
- ¼ teaspoon salt

How To

1. Take a frying pan and place it over medium heat

2. Add sliced bacon and cook until they have a crispy texture

3. Take a microwave proof container and mix all of the listed ingredients (including cooked bacon), clean the sides

4. Microwave for 75 seconds making to put your microwave to high power

5. Take out the cup and slam it against a surface to take the cake out

6. Garnish with a bit of jalapeno and serve!

Nutrition (Per Serving)

- Calories: 429
- Fat: 38g
- Carbohydrates: 6g

- Protein: 16g

Fluffy Chocolate Mousse

Serving: 4
Prep Time: 5 minutes
Cook Time: Nil
Ingredients
- 1 can (14.5 ounces) coconut cream, chilled
- 3 tablespoons unsweetened cocoa powder
- ¼ cup Swerve
- 1 teaspoon vanilla extract

How To
1. Take a large-sized mixing bowl and add coconut cream, whip with a hand mixer
2. Keep whipping for 3 minutes until fluffy
3. Fold in cocoa powder, vanilla, swerve and mix
4. Serve immediately!

Nutrition (Per Serving)
- Calories: 222
- Fat: 22g
- Carbohydrates: 4g
- Protein: 1g

The Coconut Loaf

Serving: 4
Prep Time: 15 minutes
Cook Time: 40 minutes
Ingredients
- 1 and ½ tablespoons coconut flour
- ¼ teaspoon baking powder
- 1/8 teaspoon salt
- 1 tablespoon coconut oil, melted
- 1 whole egg

How To
1. Preheat your oven to 350 degrees F
2. Add coconut flour, baking powder, salt
3. Add coconut oil, eggs and stir well until mixed
4. Leave the batter for several minutes

5. Pour half batter onto a baking pan
6. Spread it to form a circle, repeat with remaining batter
7. Bake in the oven for 10 minutes
8. Once a golden brown texture comes, let it cool and serve
9. Enjoy!

Nutrition (Per Serving)
- Calories: 297
- Fat: 14g
- Carbohydrates: 15g
- Protein: 15g

Hearty Almond Bread

Serving: 8
Prep Time: 15 minutes
Cook Time: 60 minutes
Ingredients

- 3 cups almond flour
- 1 teaspoon baking soda
- 2 teaspoons baking powder
- ¼ teaspoon salt
- ¼ cup almond milk
- ½ cup + 2 tablespoons olive oil
- 3 whole eggs

How To

1. Preheat your oven to 300 degrees F
2. Take a 9x5 inch loaf pan and grease, keep it on the side
3. Add listed ingredients to a bowl and pour the batter into the loaf pan
4. Bake for 60 minutes
5. Once baked, remove from oven and let it cool
6. Slice and serve!

Nutrition (Per Serving)

- Calories: 277
- Fat: 21g
- Carbohydrates: 7g
- Protein: 10g

Egg And Coconut Bread

Serving: 4
Prep Time: 15 minutes
Cook Time: 40 minutes

Ingredients

- 4 whole eggs
- 1 cup of water
- 2 tablespoons apple cider vinegar
- ¼ cup + 1 teaspoon coconut oil, melted
- ½ teaspoon garlic powder
- ½ cup coconut flour

- ½ teaspoon baking soda
- ¼ teaspoon Coarse salt

How To

1. Preheat your oven to 350 degrees F
2. Grease a baking tin with 1 teaspoon coconut oil, keep it on the side
3. Add eggs to blender alongside water, vinegar, ¼ cup coconut oil, blend for half a minute
4. Add garlic powder, baking soda, coconut flour, salt and blend for a minute
5. Transfer to the baking tin
6. Bake for 40 minutes
7. Serve and enjoy!

Nutrition (Per Serving)

- Calories: 297
- Fat: 14g
- Carbohydrates: 16g
- Protein: 15g

Spicy Bread Loaf

Serving: 4-6
Prep Time: 15 minutes
Cook Time: 55 minutes
Ingredients

- 6 big whole eggs
- 3 big jalapenos
- 4 ounces of turkey bacon
- ½ cup ghee
- ¼ teaspoon baking soda
- ¼ teaspoon salt
- ½ cup coconut flour

How To

1. Preheat your oven to 400 degrees F
2. Cut 3 big jalapenos and cut the jalapenos in slices, cut turkey bacon into thick slices
3. Place jalapenos and bacon on the baking tray, roast for 30 minutes
4. Flip ad bake for 5 minutes more
5. Remove seeds from jalapeno and add jalapeno and bacon slices to a food processor
6. Take a big bowl and add eggs, ghee, ¼ cup water

7. Mix well and add coconut flour, baking soda, salt and stir
8. Add jalapeno and bacon mix
9. Use a bit of ghee to grease the loaf pan
10. Pour batter into loaf pan
11. Bake for 40 minutes
12. Enjoy

Nutrition (Per Serving)

- Calories: 240
- Fat: 20g
- Carbohydrates: 5g
- Protein: 9g

Conclusion

I can't express how honored I am to think that you found my book entertaining and informative enough to read it all through to the end.

From here on out, I would encourage you to keep experimenting with different ingredients and walk towards the path of becoming the next master of the arts of meal prep with your personal Diet program!

I thank you again for purchasing this book, and I hope that you had as much fun reading it as I had writing it.

If you loved the contents, please make sure to leave feedback as it would encourage me to move forward and create more quality content for you!

Printed by Amazon Italia Logistica S.r.l.
Torrazza Piemonte (TO), Italy